101 Things to Make
for Fun or Money

By MIRIAM MORRISON PEAKE

Illustrated by JUNE FERGUSON NICOL
Cover photo by MILTON CHARLES

SCHOLASTIC BOOK SERVICES
NEW YORK · TORONTO · LONDON · AUCKLAND · SYDNEY

A Thank-you Note

Few books are ever completed without the help
and encouragement of others. In this case, an ex-
pression of gratitude is due the many people who
contributed materials and ideas, especially
Patricia Quigley, Ellen Yard, and Polly Webster.

MIRIAM MORRISON PEAKE

5th printing ....September 1969

Printed in the U.S.A.

Contents

TRADE SECRETS

Whatever you make, whether to give or to sell, is designed to bring pleasure to someone. Unless it is well planned and well made, your time and money are thrown away. No matter how small, trivial, or inexpensive, it should be unusual, eye-catching, and attractive. It should also be either useful or fun.

Do plan on making something that isn't available in the stores, or on adding a personal touch. Handmade luxuries are expensive to buy; perhaps you could make them for very little, investing your time instead of your money. Make "fun" things; start a fad if you can.

In this book there are dozens of suggestions for things you can make, but it is up to you to decide what your friends would like, or what will sell in your community.

In order for your handiwork to make a hit with your friends or the general public, consider the following points.

Excellence

Whatever you make must be *good*. Glued things should stick together; sewing must be neat, with firm seams and fine stitches; painted decorations have to be meticulously applied. *Whether you make a dozen items as personal gifts, or ten dozen items to sell, each one should be as perfect as the first.* When you give carelessly made presents, you are being discourteous to your family and friends. If you offer inferior items for sale, they will be promptly returned as unsatisfactory!

Style

There are styles in decoration, colors, and materials, as well as in clothes. When a style has flooded the market, it is on its way out. What *everybody* is wearing or using or buying today is apt to look out of date tomorrow.

Anticipate new trends. Read the topnotch fashion and home-decorating magazines. Get into the mood of what is happening now, so that you can begin to predict what is going to happen next. If this season's reds are orangy, probably blue-red will be popular next season. When short evening gowns have been done to death, watch for a change to floor-length skirts. Although Paris designers keep their new ideas top secret, most of the styles look pretty much the same when they are finally presented. Why? Because the fashion experts have all anticipated the same trends!

Appeal

That vague "something" that makes puppy dogs and baby chicks irresistible, that makes one sweater a favorite or causes everyone to prefer a certain corner of the sofa, is known as appeal, and has several ingredients that can be pinned down.

1. *Convenient Size.* Puppy dogs and baby chicks are small and easy to hold. That sweater fits especially well. The favor-

ite couch corner seems just the right size for curling up with a book.

2. *Texture*. Puppies and baby chicks are soft and downy, and people like soft, warm, fluffy things — silky furs, angora mittens, cashmere sweaters. They also like smooth, crisp textures, especially in summer.

So there may also be a *seasonal texture appeal:* fluffy, soft, and warm in cold weather; crisp, cool, and smooth in hot weather.

Besides the actual temperature appeal, there is an *anticipation appeal*. As fall and winter approach, people like to get ready for the invigorating days ahead; as winter gives way to spring, they grow tired of heavy clothing and look forward eagerly to warm weather. Fur coats are taken out of storage during Indian summer, and Easter hats appear before the last snow has melted.

3. *Proportion*. Things must balance — is that hat top-heavy? Are those painted flowers too small and insignificant on that big canister? Does one building look too squat, while another gives the impression that a strong gale might topple it? There are rules for good proportion, but you can probably tell by instinct when proper balance is achieved. *Exaggerated proportions* can also be used effectively *if they are exaggerated on purpose*. Look at Walt Disney's animals. They certainly aren't copies of real animals; their heads and feet are too big and their ears are enormous. Mr. Disney has noticed the proportions that make baby rabbits more appealing than full-grown ones, and has exaggerated them with great success.

4. *Detail*. Sometimes detail is only a neatly bound edge, or the good ribbon on a baby bonnet. *If your design is supposed to be simple, keep it simple.* But if you are making something ornate, plan each bit of decoration as carefully as you would paint a picture. *Never add any haphazard or meaningless extras to clutter up your basic design.* Don't put a crocheted edge or some embroidered flowers on a cheap handkerchief; instead, do hand hemstitching on fine linen. Examine expensive merchandise in the better stores and you will see that good taste, good materials, and careful workmanship bring the highest prices!

5. *Comfort*. A beach hat that stays firmly anchored in the wind is preferable to one that teeters with the slightest motion. A down pillow is softer than a pillow with synthetic padding. The neckband of a sweater should slide easily over the head.

6. *Usefulness*. A tote bag that will carry anything, from one book to a week's groceries, is more practical than a bag designed only for one pair of shoes. A potholder must be well insulated and big enough so that it really protects the hand from a sizzling casserole.

7. *Durability*. People expect things to last a reasonable length of time. The hand stenciling on dishtowels should be washable. The decorations should stay on matchboxes as long as the matches last.

When you have learned the importance of these qualities, you will be a discriminating shopper, as well as a potential young designer.

IDEAS
UNLIMITED

G O SHOPPING. Does your neighborhood have a "boutique"? This is pronounced *boo-teek,* and is a small shop or a special gift department that carries expensive and unusual gifts. Look over the items offered for sale; perhaps they will suggest things *you* could make or decorate. Wander through houseware and specialty shops. Examine the counters in a chain store — what simple objects do you see that you could embellish and turn into little luxuries?

You aren't going to copy anything! Just get into the mood so your own imagination will start working.

Read the shopping columns. Collect gift catalogues. Leaf through the how-to sections of family magazines, especially the July, November, and December issues (your library probably has old editions). Ask the librarian to help you locate books and articles on arts and crafts. Write for manufacturers' free instruction leaflets.

Train Your Imagination

The more you use your imagination, the more it will grow. Designers are frequently asked why they never run out of ideas. The usual answer is: "Why, everything I see and hear gives me inspiration. The trouble is that I get so many ideas I never have enough time to use them all!"

Here is your first exercise: Look over the simple objects in your house with fresh eyes. Do any of them suggest an idea? Could you turn one of them into a pretty gift item or use it for a completely different purpose?

Take a commonplace flowerpot, for instance. Write down three things you could do with it:

1. _____

2. _____

3. _____

Did you fill in all the spaces? Did you think of several ways to decorate it, perhaps a few other uses for it? On page 13 you will find several suggestions.

Now it's your turn. See how many ideas you can develop on your own. Pick at least three more common objects and try to write down half a dozen ways to decorate them, and perhaps another purpose for which they can be used. Are your designs different? Are they practical? Could *you* do them?

Experiment with Color

Be adventurous! Get some discarded color cards of yarns, fabrics, and paints from your local stores, snippets of bright-colored materials, different colored threads; cut out colors from magazine pictures. Mix them up. Make unusual groupings. Try turquoise with orange, rust, brown, olive green, lemon yellow, or pale blue. Does it make an exciting color scheme or does it look awful? Suddenly, two colors you never thought would blend will create a magnificent effect. Clip these samples together so you won't forget them. Keep on experimenting until you have a dozen new and startling color combinations. Try the same thing with *more* than two colors — frequently two clashing shades can be brought into harmony by the addition of a third color.

Look for Unusual Materials

There might be stores, factories, or workshops in your neighborhood that discard scraps of leather, bits of fur or felt, rich fabric remnants, smidgins of lace or trimmings. Perhaps they would give you some of these, or let you buy them. Collect discarded costume jewelry, beads, and trimming; snippets of fabric and yarn.

Scout secondhand shops and thrift shops for bits of ivory or inlay, old feather fans and furs. Ask the wallpaper dealer for discontinued samples or damaged pieces. Your electrician probably has short lengths of copper wire he no longer needs. Use these things for your experiments. Figure the cost if you have to buy them — you want to save as much as possible when you are making gifts; later on, if you decide to start your own business, you will have to shop for them, so find out costs and make sure of a source of supply.

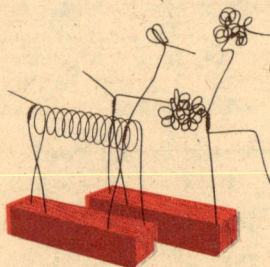

Find Things to Decorate

There are hundreds of things you can decorate, and dozens of different methods to use. Try out various techniques to see which one suits you best; practice on something old or worthless before you try to ornament anything of value.

Be Patient. It may take several attempts before you develop skill and things turn out well. If you are stymied by one method, even after you have given it a fair chance, take a shot at something else. *There is bound to be something you can master and will enjoy doing.*

Be Daring. Decorate amusing things, make "conversation pieces." In case you decide to start a business later on, remember that such silly things as jeweled fly swatters, whisk brooms, and dustpans, mink-trimmed ball-point pens, even wooden back-scratchers with fur bracelets and rhinestone rings, have sold by the thousands in topnotch stores, and earned a pretty penny for somebody. Stocking stuffers for Christmas are hard to find (adults as well as children often hang up their stockings), so anything attractive that would fit a slim stocking and a slim budget would be snapped up.

Decide on Your Technique. Different items call for different types of decorations. After you know which method is best for you, select the things that can be suitably decorated with your specialty. If you want to beautify a wastepaper basket, paint or a paste pot is indicated. If you like to sew, then appliqué, embroidery, or beading is your dish. Why not try a few experiments that combine different techniques? You may find a brand-new way that appeals to you!

Develop Several Ideas

You never know what you can make successfully until you try. Besides, you don't want to give everybody on your list identical presents. Even if you want to make nothing but aprons, no two need be alike; vary the colors, the trimmings, the styles. Some can be smartly tailored for practical use; others can be pure glamor — sequin-trimmed organdy or even velvet with ostrich feathers! If there are men and boys on your list, you may want to make gifts for them, possibly a barbecue or carpenter's apron. How about trying a completely different present, such as finely wrought cuff links of silver wire, a set of bookends, or a turtleneck dickey? To your surprise, one of these might prove to be better than aprons for your business venture later on.

Whether you work with scissors and glue, a pair of pliers, or a sewing machine, just be sure that your workmanship is the very best possible. When you run into a problem, there is always someone to help with advice — your home economics teacher, the proprietor of your arts or crafts shop, even the manufacturer whose products you use. The companies that make the sewing machine, the yarn, the glue, or the silver wire have experts who will answer your letters.

Look to a Bright Future

Each technique you master is bound to come in handy some day. When you have a home of your own, it may help you to be your own decorator.

Skill in one handicraft builds skill in others. The ability to express yourself with any creative work brings satisfaction, pleasure, sometimes even a future career.

Flowerpot Ideas

Here are the suggestions we promised you on page 9.

1. Cover one with mosaic tiles. Use small tiles that will fit easily around the curves and the tapered sides. You may have to cut some of the tiles to fit.

2. Spray one with gold paint, deck with fake jewels and gold braid, fill with plastic foam and plant a spray of artificial flowers.

3. Decorate a small one with glitter and use it as a base for a round pincushion.

4. Paint one to be used as a pencil holder.

5. Make a topiary tree in a gilded flowerpot (see page 87).

6. Little brightly painted flowerpots can be filled with party favors or planted with lollipop flowers in a plastic foam ball for children's parties.

7. Cover one with floral or scenic paper, varnish it.

8. Stop up the hole in the base with cork, or cover it with adhesive plastic. Fill it with colored stones to be used as a doorstop.

Maybe you came up with some even better ideas!

GLITTER
and GLUE

DECORATING with paste or glue is called "collage." This is a French word that means, literally, pasting or paper-hanging and is pronounced *caw-lahj*. It is one of the easiest and least expensive methods of turning simple things into little luxuries.

When an artist makes a collage, he arranges pieces of paper, fragments of cloth, and various oddments until they form a pleasing effect; then glues them in place to make a "picture." He may use anything: old-fashioned valentines, advertisements, clippings, travel posters, or ticket stubs; a lace handkerchief, a bunch of dried grasses, even wire screening and machinery parts! Some collages carry out a theme — the theater, travel, the Wild West; others combine completely unrelated materials and create a bizarre effect.

Use whatever you feel will enhance your decoration: fake jewels, beads, lace, glitter, braids, fringe, ribbons, paper or fabric, feathers or fur.

The Right Adhesive

There are many kinds of glue and paste suitable for your work. Always read the instructions on the package or bottle before you buy or use one. Many are extremely inflammable, so keep them away from any open flame. A few should not be left in contact with the skin; so apply them with a brush or a disposable spreader of some kind.

Rubber cement is especially intended for paper. Coat both surfaces and let each piece dry for a moment until the cement is "tacky." This will form a permanent bond. Keep the cement thinned enough, with rubber cement thinner, so that it will spread evenly without forming lumps, but not so thin that it is watery. Any excess can be rubbed off. Save the hardened cement that accumulates at the top of the bottle where you wipe off your brush, knead it into a ball, and use it as an eraser to gather up any excess along the edges of the paper.

Glue comes in several forms. White glue in a squeeze bottle is easiest to handle, can be used for almost anything, and dries clear. It needs to be applied only to one surface, is soluble in water, and can be wiped off with a damp cloth. This glue should be spread evenly. When you use it on fabric, avoid any thick blobs that could leak through and cause spots. It dries quickly.

Glueing can be a messy business unless you work carefully. Spread out plenty of newspapers and keep a damp cloth handy for wiping your hands or cleaning up any spills. Close the bottle or tube immediately after each application, to keep the contents free-flowing. Here are some pointers to remember:

Always use glue sparingly; you can add more if you find you need it.

To apply ribbon or braid, put a dab of glue on one finger, then draw the ribbon or braid over this finger as you guide it into place.

To join the ends of padded cord, allow 1/2 inch for over-lapping ends. Remove 1/2 inch padding from each end, then overlap these ends and glue them in place. This makes an invisible joining.

To hold braid in place on an edge until the glue has dried, clamp it with clothespins or hair clips, especially if you are turning a corner.

Cement for special purposes, such as joining metal, making jewelry, or paving something with mosaic tiles, is also available. Each type can usually be bought at the store where you find craft supplies.

Varnishing

Whenever collage is used for trays, wastebaskets, bottles, or anything that is expected to last an indefinite time, it should be coated with varnish to protect it from soil, wear, and moisture. Many kinds of glue will dissolve if subjected to washing.

The easiest method of varnishing is to use a spray that will cover the surface with synthetic enamel. You can also use liquid varnish applied with a paint brush. The brush should be cleaned with turpentine. Shellac gives a nice finish, but isn't waterproof. A brush that has been used for shellac should be cleaned with alcohol.

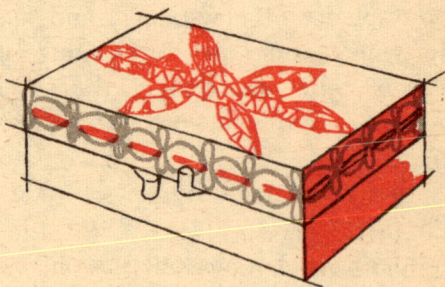

Decorated Containers

Almost any glass, plastic, or metal container that has a possible future use and good proportions, can be converted into an attractive and useful gift.

There are dozens of things to use for decoration, as you can see by the examples in this chapter: ribbons, braid, rickrack; artificial flowers and lace; sequins and fake jewels; pictures cut from magazines or catalogues; gold spray or bright paint; fabric, paper, and even buttons. Again, use your imagination and develop your own ideas.

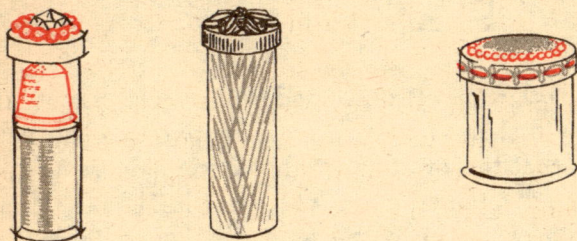

One little pill box has its lid topped with a fake jewel that is circled by pearl beads — to become a miniature sewing kit. Its twin, topped with a handsome shank button — held tight in a tiny slit — holds colored toothpicks. Still another is splashed with glitter, circled with sequins and edged with braid.

These little plastic boxes, suitable for stamps or aspirin tablets, are garnished with gold braid, large rhinestones, sequins, or artificial flowers.

A mouthwash decanter, which could be filled with hand lotion, sports three rows of decorative braid. Stopper sparkles with a rhinestone and pretend pearls.

The other one is decorated with flower cutouts that have first been pasted on decorative or plain paper (so that the printing on the wrong side won't show through), then sprayed with varnish. The bow around the neck of the bottle is made of metallic knitting ribbon; the trade name on the stopper is covered by a sequin rosette encircled with large sequins.

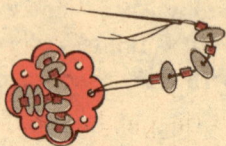

To make a sequin rosette, start with one large sequin called a "wheel of fortune." This has a scalloped edge with one hole in the center and eight holes around the edge. Starting at center with needle and thread, slip four small crystal beads and three sequins alternately on the needle, then insert needle through one hole at the edge. Working from the edge to the center, repeat this group of bead and sequins all around. The beads will hold the sequins upright to look like petals.

An inexpensive little goblet holds a corsage of fake posies. Plastic wrap, trimmed with sequins and held in place with firmly glued gold braid, covers the top. A bow of gold cord is tied around the stem.

How festive the little pin box and tape measure look wearing corsages of delicate artificial blossoms!

Decorated Matches

Matches of any kind are a suitable gift for an adult. You can decorate them by the dozens in less time than it takes to tell about it. If your time and money run short, these make wonderful last-minute presents.

Match Folders. A box of these contains about fifty folders and costs very little. One sheet of gift-wrap paper is enough to cover them all. Select a very elegant paper: metallic foil, velvety or flocked paper, small designs in beautiful colors. Avoid flimsy paper and the kind of gift wrap with large pictures or messages. Wallpaper is often suitable; striped paper in handsome colors is fine if you are careful to follow the stripes when you apply it.

Open the folders and brush them on the *outside* with rubber cement. Brush rubber cement on the *wrong side* of the paper. When both surfaces are "tacky," lay the folders, side by side, on the paper; allow 1/2 inch at the bottom of each folder near the striking surface and 2 inches at the top to be folded down inside the cover. Let them dry. Cut the folders apart, leaving the margins at top and bottom.

Brush rubber cement inside the covers and just below the striking surface. Press the margins of the paper in place, folding down the cover to make sure the paper will stretch over the fold. Trim away any excess on the edges.

When you have covered ten or twenty folders, stack them in rows with the tops facing in alternate directions on each folder. Wrap them in clear plastic film, or arrange them in a decorated box.

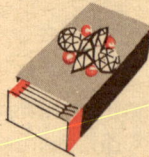

Safety Matches. There are tiny boxes and medium-sized boxes of safety matches that are sold in packages of about ten boxes. Brush rubber cement on *one* side of each matchbox and on the *wrong* side of the paper. When the cement is "tacky," place the boxes on the paper, leaving enough room between them to cut them apart; when they are dry, cut the paper between the boxes, trim away any excess on the edges. Flip them over and do the other sides.

If the paper is handsome and unusual enough to form a complete decoration, fine! Otherwise there are more exciting things to do. Collect pretty buttons, bits of ribbon, any small ornaments, discarded costume jewelry.

Drop a blob of rubber cement on top of the matchbox (open the box to make sure the matches will be right side up and won't fall out) and press the trimmings in place.

Kitchen Matches. For decorating these boxes, you need some sheets of fine sandpaper as well as an ornamental covering. They can be glamorized for use in the living room, or turned into handsome accessories for the kitchen. Cover the entire box with beautiful paper, velvet, or brocade (fabric can be sewed to the box edges instead of being pasted on); or use some of the adhesive plastic that can be bought by the roll: 1/2 yard will cover a lot of boxes. The seam, where the fabric or other covering is joined, should be on one side, over a striking surface. The seam is later covered by a piece of sandpaper cut to fit that side of the box. If you use fabric, finish the edges of the box with gold braid, gimp (upholstery braid), or narrow rickrack. You can cover the ends of the box if you wish.

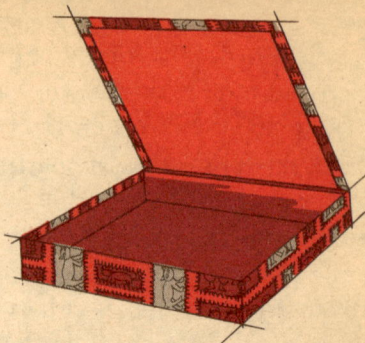

Covered Boxes

You need:

Cigar, stationery, or candy box with attached lid

About 1/2 yard decorative fabric, such as velvet, calico, brocade, or Toile de Jouy (pronounced *Twahl de Jwee*). Be sure fabric is firmly woven, not too thick for lid to close, and does not fray easily.

Glue

Place box on wrong side of material, centering any pattern; nap of velvet on lid of box should brush toward front. Allow margins large enough to cover entire outside of box, plus about 1 inch that will be turned over edges. (Diagram shows how box is placed on material; dotted lines show where excess has to be cut away *a little at a time,* as each part is completed.)

Leaving a 1-inch margin, cut material around lid, but *not quite* to base of lid. Spread glue evenly over the top of lid, smooth fabric neatly in place. Spread glue over inside edges of lid, clip corner (A), fold down top edge, and glue in place (B). Fold down corner of side margin (C) and glue this margin in place (D). This forms a mitered corner: no raw edges will show, but most of bulk has been cut away from under overlapping fabric. As an edge is glued, it can be held in place with clothespins or hair clips. Glue margin on other side of lid in same way. Next, glue fabric to back and bottom of box, and bring fabric up around front and sides, mitering each corner and glueing it in place, with 1 inch extending over edges to the inside.

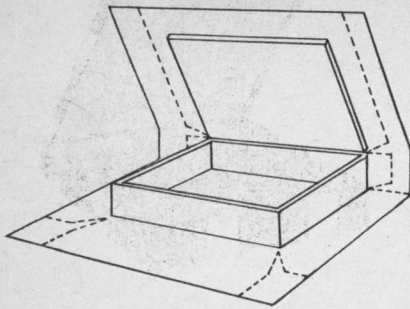

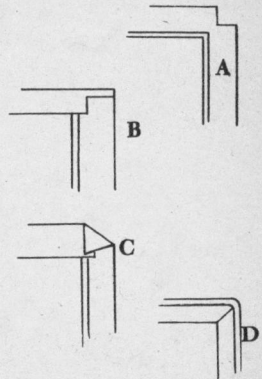

When box is completely covered, line inside with fabric or heavy paper. Cut lining by fitting it over *outside* of bottom and sides. Raw edges of fabric lining must be mitered where excess is cut away at corners: sew or glue corners together where they will meet, then cut away folds. (Edges of lining must cover raw edges of covering to within 1/4 to 1/2 inch of edges of box.) Glue lining in place.

If you use a velvet, or other solid-color fabric, the lid can be trimmed with gold braid, jewels, or gold-paper ornaments.

More Ideas. Decorate sturdy cardboard gift boxes for hosiery, gloves, handkerchiefs, lingerie, and similar items, with pretty paper and strips of braid, lace, rickrack, or bunches of flowers. Decorate hat boxes and dress boxes to be used for storing things on closet shelves. Decorate boxes that would make convenient containers for cosmetics and other small items in bureau drawers. Notice the sizes of plain gift boxes for sale: you might even buy some of these and trim them.

Felt-covered Notebook

You need:
School notebook, 7½ by 9½ inches
3/8 yard felt
2½ yards gold cord
Gold-paper ornament
Glue

Spread glue evenly on the front cover. Allowing felt to extend slightly beyond edges of notebook, press felt firmly in place. Spread glue over rest of the cover and press on felt. When glue is dry, trim away felt margins.

Cut gold cord in half. Pin two ends to edge of notebook, halfway between front and back covers. Put a dab of glue on one finger, draw cords over glue, and press evenly along the edge to the first corner. Clamp cords at corner with a clothespin or hair clip. Continue glueing cords around edges and clamping them at corners until they reach the pinned ends. Allowing ½ inch for overlap, cut cords. Remove padding from all four ends of cords. Overlap ends, and glue them to form an invisible joining. Glue ornament to center of front cover.

Matching Pencil Holder. Use an empty fruit-juice can or other small can. Wash and dry it thoroughly and make sure it has no sharp or jagged edges. Spray the inside with gold paint. Cover the outside with felt, joining edges neatly without overlapping them. Glue double cord around top of can; glue ornament to front, opposite seam.

Matchbox. Glue felt to top and bottom of box. Glue ornament to center top.

24

More Ideas. Cover an address book, small notebooks for memos, and small boxes in the same way. Cover a ledger with felt, then glue two velvet ribbons lengthwise on the front cover, leaving a long end on one ribbon extending toward the top. This extra ribbon is then brought down inside the ledger as a bookmark. Cover a loose-leaf notebook for recipes with marbleized adhesive plastic.

For a man, cover a small address book and matching pocket notebook with handsome imitation leather and omit any trimming.

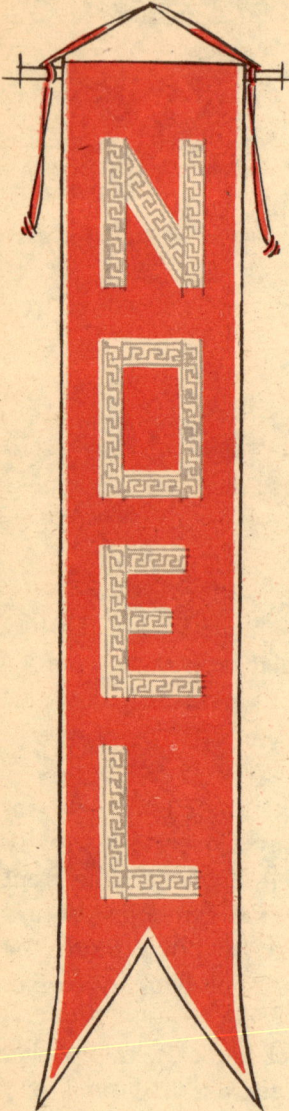

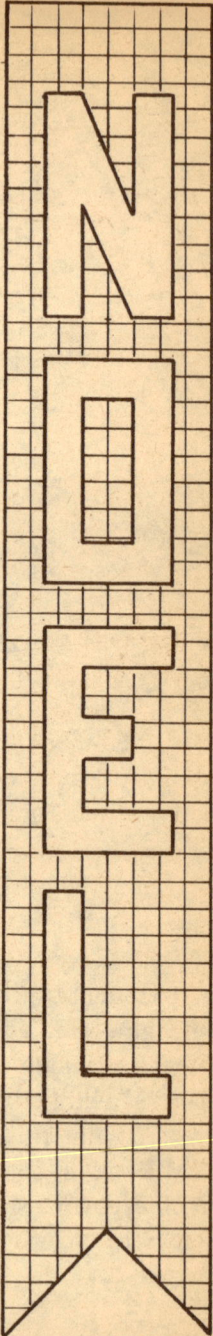

Noel Pennant

You need:

    Strip of blue felt, 8 by 50 inches
    10-inch wooden dowel
    2½ yards gold and white ribbon, 7/8 inch wide
    3½ yards gold braid, 1/4 inch wide
    Gold spray paint
    Glue

Make sure that all edges on felt are straight and even. To cut notched end of pennant, make a pencil mark 4 inches from one end and 4 inches from side edge. Draw diagonal lines from this mark to each corner. Cut along these lines.

Each square on chart represents 1 inch. The first letter starts 3½ inches below top edge and is 1½ inches from sides. With chalk, outline each letter, following measurements on chart. Allowing 1/2 inch for turning under raw ends, cut a length of ribbon for each section of first letter. Turn under 1/4 inch at both ends of one length and glue these little hems; then glue ribbon in place on chalk outlines. Continue in this way until all letters have been glued to pennant.

Mark off 2 inches at top edge for hem. Starting across base of hem, glue braid around edges of pennant (pages 15-16). Spray dowel with gold paint. Fold hem over dowel and glue securely. Tie a 16-inch length of gold braid to ends of dowel for hanging pennant.

More Ideas. Decorate a white pennant with a garland of Christmas greens, cutting the leaves from green felt and using pompons from red ball fringe for the berries. Make a red pennant with a string of Christmas ornaments: cut the ornaments out of white felt and trim each one with sequins, rhinestones, and gold braid (see Christmas stocking on page 55). Glue a tall felt Christmas tree to a white pennant, trim it with miniature decorations; or make a felt topiary tree, similar to the one on page 87, and trim it with red ribbon and artificial flowers.

Christmas-tree Ornaments

You need:
  Plastic foam balls
  Ribbons or gold braid; rhinestones, sequins, pail-
    lettes, pearl beads, or other ornaments
  Glue and pins

Divide ball into quarters with braid or ribbon, having the
ends meet at the center top. Fasten ribbons and braid with
glue or pins. Continue adding braid or ribbon; ball may be
completely covered, or the ribbons spaced evenly around. Tie
the last ribbon in a bow at top. Glue or pin ornaments in place.
Attach a hook, or a loop of ribbon or cord for hanging ornament to tree.

More Ideas. Roll the balls in glue, then in glitter. Spray with
varnish to keep the glitter in place. Stud completely with
sequins, pearls, and fake jewels, pinned in place; always divide
ball into quarters when you start, to keep decorations evenly
spaced. Gild with gold spray paint, then decorate. Trim some
with bright red artificial flowers and green leaves, tie green
velvet ribbons around them, and pin the ribbons firmly in
place.

Easter Eggs

You need:
  Foam-plastic eggs or blown eggshells
  Ribbons, sequins, gold braid, fake jewels, tiny arti-
    ficial flowers
  Glue

To blow an eggshell, pierce both ends of egg with a sharp
needle. *Gently* enlarge hole at large end of egg by inserting a
hatpin or skewer and working it around. Be sure to pierce the
yolk. Place the large hole over a bowl and blow into small hole

until all the egg has been re-moved. Rinse empty shell with clear water. Glue ribbon or braid around egg, dividing it in half or quarters. Trim with various ornaments, glueing them in place. If egg is to be hung up, tie ribbon in a bow and leave enough for a loop at the top, or add a loop of gold cord. The finished egg can be spray-varnished.

More Ideas. Color or gild the eggs before you trim them. Paint faces on eggshells, make lace-paper doilies into ruffled collars to hold them upright, then glue on yarn hair, paper or flower hats, lace bonnets trimmed with ribbon and flowers. Paint pink noses and eyes, and attach white paper whiskers and rabbit ears, lined with pink. Set them on large marshmallows as favors for children's parties. Paint eggshells or hard-boiled eggs in decorative patterns, then add a few sequins.

Jack Horner Pie

You need:
> Cardboard paint bucket
> 3 packages of fire-resistant crêpe paper, one each of
>   green, orange, and yellow
> 3 packages of gift ribbon to match
> 12 inexpensive toys or favors
> Rubber cement

Unwrap crêpe paper and open it up to its full length. Turn bucket upside down on one end of the orange paper and draw a circle around edge of bucket. Allowing 3 inches all around this circle, cut it out and set it aside.

Cut three strips of orange paper 4 inches wide, three strips yellow 5 inches wide and three strips of green 6 inches wide, the entire length of paper. Fold orange strips with ends meeting, then fold again several times and cut one edge to form petals about 2 inches wide and 2½ inches deep. Cut petals on yellow strips slightly larger; cut even larger petals on two green strips; on the third green strip cut pointed leaf shapes.

Brush rubber cement around top of bucket and wrap first orange strip around and around it, with petals extending beyond rim. Continue brushing on rubber cement and wrapping orange strips so that they cover one third of the bucket; stretch the crêpe paper enough to keep strips flat against bucket. The petals will be inclined to turn down, so push them up as you wrap.

Cover next third of bucket with yellow strips, and last third of bucket with green strips, pasting leaf-shaped strips last.

Tie each toy to a 1-yard length of ribbon and place it inside bucket. Cut twelve small slits in orange circle that was set aside, and cut the 3-inch margin into petals. Draw the ribbons through the slits. Brush top rim of bucket with rubber cement and press the circle in place to cover top. Stretch out petals.

Velvet-trimmed Mirror

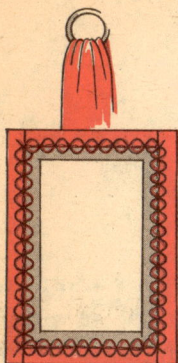

You need:

Framed mirror, 6 by 8 inches

1 yard each velvet ribbon 1/2 inch wide, in two shades of one color

3/8 yard velvet ribbon in matching color, 2 inches wide

Brass curtain ring

1 yard gold braid

Glue

If back of the frame is flatter than the front, take out mirror. Reverse frame and use flat side. Allowing 1 inch at each end, cut lengths of ribbon for each side of frame. Glue one color to outer edge of frame, carrying the ends over edge of frame to the wrong side. Glue other color in the same way to inner edges of frame. Glue mirror to frame, then cover joining of mirror and frame on the right side with gold braid. Loop wide ribbon through brass ring and glue at least 2 inches of both ends to back of mirror, making sure that it is attached firmly enough to hold weight of mirror.

This type of mirror is ideal to hang on the back of a coat-closet door, or on the wall near a desk or dressing table.

More Ideas. Frame a small handbag mirror with one row of narrow velvet ribbon and one row of narrow gold braid. Add a loop of ribbon for hanging mirror on the wall. Make a case of wide velvet ribbon to hold a purse-size mirror. To hold a color picture, cover a small oval frame with fake jewels and pearl beads; it will resemble a painted miniature! Make a cardboard frame for a picture and trim it with velvet and pearls.

SOMETHING to SEW

SEWING IS AN ACCOMPLISHMENT that will repay you many times over for any effort you invest. As you try out various techniques, you will be increasing your skills and diversifying your interests.

This chapter suggests ideas for machine or hand sewing. Most of them are quick and easy to do, a few are more ambitious; some are practical, others pure glamor.

Included are several basic embroidery stitches that even a beginner can master. A touch of embroidery will often turn a piece of plain sewing into a cherished possession.

So thread your needle — or your sewing machine — and get ready to begin!

Heart Pincushion

You need:
> Small piece of red felt
> 1/2 yard gold braid and 1/2 yard gold cord
> Synthetic wadding
> Pins

Cut two pieces of felt in a heart shape. Remember that when cushion has been filled, it will appear smaller. Sew pieces together, leaving an opening. Insert wadding and sew opening. Trim edge with gold braid, sew a loop of gold cord to top. Make design of pins in center of cushion.

Fish Pincushion

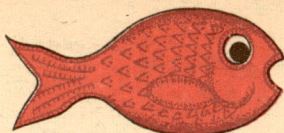

You need:
2 pieces of yellow or green felt
Dark-green embroidery floss
2 "moving eyes" or large sequins
Synthetic wadding
Pins

Draw outline of fish on paper. Remember that when fish cushion is filled, it will appear smaller and thinner. Cut out drawing and trace outline on both pieces of felt. Using three strands of floss, embroider outlines of eye, gill, and fin in blanket stitch (see pages 58-60 for embroidery stitches). Embroider scales with fly stitches and work one row outline stitch around mouth. Using blanket stitch, join the two pieces, leaving an opening at center back. Insert wadding, then close opening with blanket stitch. Sew on "moving eye" (these can be bought where you buy sequins) or sequin. Insert pins in spaces between blanket stitches around gill and fin, then put a pin in center of each fly-stitch scale.

More Ideas. Pincushions can be made in any shape: square, round, oval, or to represent animals, fruits or vegetables, and other objects. Make them out of cotton, satin, or any fabric; trim them with braid, ribbon, rickrack, embroidery, or flowers. Be sure to use wadding that pins can be inserted into easily. Mount little pincushions by glueing them into pretty boxes, tiny flowerpots (see page 13), egg cups, or other holders. Attach an elastic bracelet to a small pincushion so that it can be worn on the wrist while sewing. Make felt needle case and attach to a pincushion.

Case for Eyeglasses or Sun Goggles

You need:

> Piece of felt 6 by 7 inches and trimming *or* leatherette or suede and machine needle for stitching leather

Felt case. Fold felt in half lengthwise to measure 3 by 7 inches and curve both ends slightly. (Use pinking or scalloping shears, if you have them, for cutting edges.) Trim one side with artificial flowers, velvet bows, or sequins and beads. These can be sewed on or glued. Fold case in half as before and stitch one side and one end. Sew a snap fastener to other end to keep glasses from sliding out.

Leatherette case. Fold and cut same as felt with plain scissors. Stitch one end and side with machine needle for leather. No trimming is needed.

More Ideas. Make cases for compacts and lipsticks, playing cards or packs of cigarettes; small cases shaped like envelopes to hold make-up, small packages of facial tissues, or notebook and pencil. Trim them with flowers, glitter, iron-on cutouts, felt cutouts, rickrack, braid, or embroidery.

34

Embroidered Burlap Apron

You need:

> 5/8 yard blue burlap, 1 yard wide
> 2½ yards gold grosgrain ribbon, 1½ inches wide
> 1/3 ounce each white, gold, and navy knitting worsted
> Rug needle

Make 1-inch hems on short edges of burlap, and a 4-inch hem on one long edge. Gather other long edge to measure 18 inches. Cut a piece of ribbon 70 inches long, and sew center of this ribbon over gathered edge on right side of apron for waistband and ties. Turning under 1 inch at each end, sew remaining ribbon on the wrong side of waistband to cover raw edges on the inside and give waistband more body.

Embroider flowers with a double strand of knitting worsted to form an uneven pyramid at center front, then add a couple of flowers on each side. Each flower is made of five lazy daisy stitches (page 59), each about 1½ inches long. Alternate the colors for each flower, then make a French knot (page 59) at center.

Orange Potholder

You need:

1/4 yard orange, 1/8 yard green cotton material
1/4 yard quilted padding
Orange and green sewing thread

Cut two circles of orange and one circle of padding 8 inches in diameter. Place both orange circles together with padding on top. Leaving 2 inches open at top edge, stitch 1/2 inch from edge, joining all three thicknesses. Trim away seam allowance of padding. Reach between the two orange circles and turn right side out. Press. Make paper pattern for leaf group as shown, having each leaf 4 inches long. Cut four pieces of green from pattern. Leaving 1½-inch opening, sew two sections together; turn right side out. Sew opening. With green thread, stitch around edges and down center of each leaf. Make other group of leaves in same way for other side. Cut strip of green 1½ inches wide and 6 inches long for stem loop. Fold long edges toward center; then bring folds together, hiding raw edges inside. Insert magnets if desired. Stitch. Pin ends of loop and leaves to top of potholder, concealing opening. Stitch in place. Make star-shaped "bud" directly opposite stem, with rows of green stitching.

Here are some basic rules: Everything should be washable, shrinkproof and colorfast: fabric, padding, and trimming. Padding must be thick enough to protect hands from a hot iron skillet or boiling pot; size should be at least 7 to 8 inches at widest part. Each potholder needs a small loop or metal ring, so that it can be hung up; as an extra bonus, slip two small magnets inside fabric loop, or attach magnets inside one corner (one on each side of the padding), so that potholder can be hung against stove.

More Ideas. Attractive ready-made potholders or oven mitts are hard to find, and since there is no limit to the kinds you can design, these should top your list. Make potholders in all shapes of fruits and vegetables; make square or round ones decorated with rickrack, braid, embroidery, even rhinestones. Make oven mitts shaped like puppets or animal heads.

Chapel Cap

You need:
  1 yard lace 2½ inches wide
  1 yard matching edging

Cut a circle of paper 9 inches in diameter. Matching lace patterns, sew two strips of wide lace together for 9 inches across center of paper circle. Cut off excess. Sew another piece of lace on each side to cover the rest of the paper. Cut off excess lace again. Pin edging around circle, covering raw edges of lace. Sew through paper, turning under ends of edging where they meet. Tear away paper.

More Ideas. Using a commercial pattern to cut the paper, make a lace vestee, a set of collar and cuffs, or even a sleeveless evening blouse.

Large Sachet

You need:
  Cotton-backed satin
  Gold braid, fancy or velvet ribbon
  Synthetic or cotton wadding
  Sachet powder

Fold satin to measure desired size of bureau drawer or suit-case. Cut off excess, crease fold. Sew ribbon or braid across both ends of one side. Fold again, wrong side out. Leaving an opening for inserting wadding, stitch other three sides and all four corners. Cut two pieces of wadding to fit sachet, sprinkle one piece with sachet powder (don't be stingy!), cover with other piece, and insert in sachet. Turning under raw edges, blindstitch opening.

Large sachets for lining bureau drawers, covering lingerie or the contents of a suitcase, make unusual gifts.

More Ideas. Make a large sachet for a bride: use white satin trim with gold braid and lace or a bunch of lilies of the valley. Make large sachets of velvet or brocade remnants. Make square sachets of satin ribbon, 4 inches wide; tie them together with narrow ribbon and top with a bunch of small arti-ficial flowers. Make heart-shaped sachets of white satin for a bride, or of pink satin for valentines; bell-shaped ones for Christmas; flower-shaped ones, adding rows of ribbon "petals," for other occasions. Sew two large, flat silk flowers together, with wadding and sachet powder between.

Teardrop Tote Bag

You need:
  5/8 yard bright-colored burlap
  5/8 yard cotton for lining
  Small amount of knitting worsted in four flower
    colors and two shades of green
  Rug needle

For bag pattern, cut paper 13 inches wide and 19 inches
long. Cut a piece of paper in a circle 13 inches across, and use
this to draw bottom curve. Mark off 4 inches at center top;
then draw a curve, as shown on diagram, from side of circle
to first mark at top. Fold pattern in half lengthwise and cut
both sides the same. Using paper pattern and allowing 1/2
inch for seams, cut out two pieces of burlap and two pieces of
lining, on straight of goods.

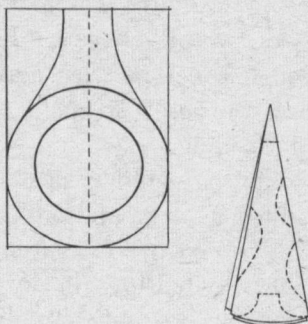

For embroidery pattern, draw a 6-inch circle on a piece of
paper. Cut out this circle and fold it in half, then in half again,
until it will form sixteen equal sections. Now cut this folded
piece as shown by dotted lines on small diagram. Open it up
and pin it in the exact center of one rounded part of burlap.
Trace all outlines carefully with pencil. Now turn to pages
58-60 for embroidery stitches.

Embroider center with a ring of blanket stitch. Each bud is a lazy daisy stitch made with a double strand of yarn. Base of each bud is made with three fly stitches. Use the same two colors for each of the single buds, and the other two colors for the buds that are directly over each other. With lighter green, make another fly stitch below each single bud, and make stems with straight stitches. Embroider outer edge with two rows of fly stitches, using lighter green for inner row and making a straight stitch between each fly stitch. Use darker green for outer row. Make one dark-green French knot in center.

Pin both pieces of burlap together, wrong side out. Stitch across top, skip 8 inches on each side, and stitch around lower part. Assemble lining in same way. Press seams. Turn burlap pieces right side out and insert lining. Folding under seam allowance, blindstitch lining to burlap around openings.

More Ideas. Make a plain tote bag of awning material, ticking, denim, or sailcloth. Leave untrimmed, or trim with braid or rickrack.

Triangular Tote Bag

You need:
1/2 yard bright-colored burlap
1/2 yard cotton lining in another color 36 inches wide
Several yards of knitting worsted in five or six colors
Rug needle

Cut two pieces of burlap 18 inches square. Mark center at top edge. Starting 4 inches from center, draw a diagonal line from top edge to bottom corner. Cut along this line, then cut other side to correspond. Cut two pieces of lining same as burlap.

Embroidery. Using a compass or a saucer, draw a 6-inch circle on paper. Fold in four to find center. Cut circle along one fold to center. Now fold the circle in three equal sections (diagram) by bringing cut edges to meet folds, then fold in three again to make nine sections. Outline a petal on each section as shown by dotted lines. Cut along these petal outlines

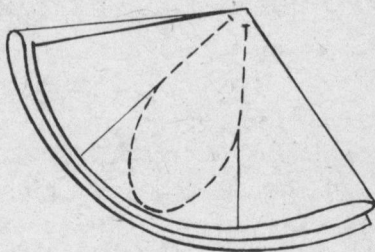

and pin paper to center of a burlap piece, 8 inches from bottom edge. Draw outline of petals with colored pencil. Make a paper pattern, 3½ inches long and 2 inches wide, for leaves. Draw outlines of leaves and stem as shown in picture. Using a different color yarn for each section of flower and leaves, embroider them as suggested (embroidery stitches are described on pages 58-60).

Center of flower is a circle filled with French knots. This is surrounded by two circles of fly stitches made in base of petals. Work outline stitch around petals and a row of fly stitches down the center of each petal. Outline leaves with blanket stitch, work a row of outline stitch next, then make two sunbursts of straight stitches in center of each leaf. Stem is embroidered in chain stitch with a row of outline stitch along one side.

Place the two pieces of burlap with right sides together. Sew top and bottom edges, taking in 1/2-inch seams; then sew sides from wide end to within 8 inches of top. Sew lining together in same way. Press seams. Turn burlap right side out and insert lining in bag. Turn under seam allowance of burlap and lining around openings, and sew together.

More Ideas. Use felt to make tote bags; these will need no linings. Trim with braid, rickrack, felt cutouts, or designs cut from iron-on tape. Make terry-cloth beach bags with plastic linings; trim with sea shells.

Chef's Apron

You need:

Butcher's apron
1/4 yard brown muslin for pocket
4 skeins embroidery floss in light green, dark green,
    red, and yellow

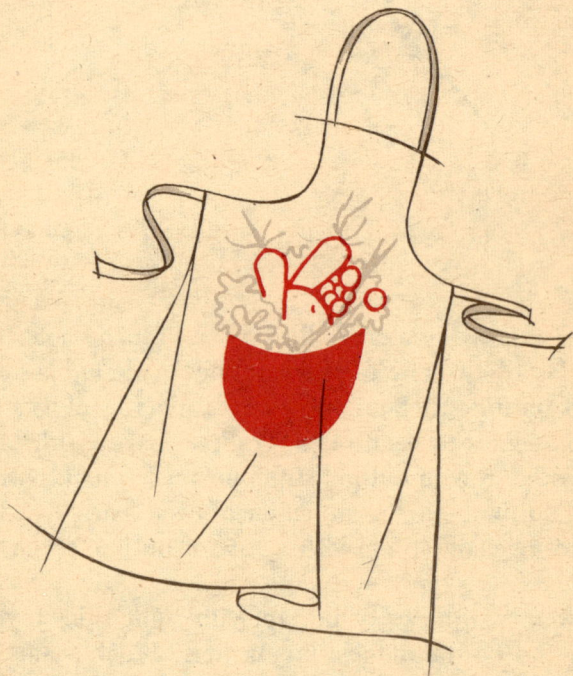

Draw a design for pocket and vegetables on paper. Make
pocket large enough to be practical — at least 7 inches wide
and about 6 inches deep. If you have trouble drawing vegetables or a substitute, such as fruit or flowers, trace them from
labels on canned foods, seed catalogues, or magazine advertisements; you can even trace them directly around real vegetables. Cut out each drawing, and arrange them all to form a

pleasing effect that will fit above the bowl pocket. Lettuce to fill in "salad" is merely made with curves and squiggles. When you are satisfied with the arrangement, anchor pieces in place with transparent tape or rubber cement.

Trace arrangement of vegetables on one piece of paper, pocket on another. Put tracings on the shiny side of carbon paper and go over the lines, transferring carbon to the back of your drawings. Next, pin drawing of vegetables on apron and go over the lines to transfer carbon to fabric. Embroider outlines in chain stitch and outline stitch (pages 58,60). The carrot tops are worked with dark-green feather-stitching. Use both shades of green for lettuce, light green for peas and scallion, and dark green for beans and radish tops.

Transfer outline of pocket to a double thickness of muslin. Allowing 1/4 inch for seams, cut out pocket, and stitch around it, leaving an opening on one side. Turn pocket right side out and stitch to apron. Press.

More Ideas. Pocket could be made of black in the shape of a top hat. Using black, embroider outline of a rabbit coming out of hat; with bright pink, add eyes, nose, inner outlines of ears, and a bow around rabbit's neck.

Another suggestion is to draw a soup-tureen pocket, tilting it slightly forward so that top forms an oval. Embroider top edge of oval, then fill oval with "tomato soup," as follows: stitch outline on a double thickness of red muslin, leaving an opening; then turn right side out and blindstitch in place. You can embroider swirls of "steam" with gray floss, brown "croutons" in the shape of little cubes, "floating" them in the soup.

Instead of embroidering the vegetables, you can cut them out of iron-on tape and iron them securely in place, following instructions on package. Or paint vegetables with fabric paint, following instructions in kit.

Poncho

You need:

1 yard heavy orange cotton material
2 yards red moss fringe
3½ yards yellow rickrack
1½ yards each green jumbo rickrack and blue giant
   rickrack
1 skein each orange, blue, and yellow embroidery
   floss

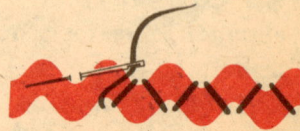

Cut two pieces of material 12½ by 36 inches. Make narrow hems on all edges. Mark three straight lines with pencil or chalk lengthwise on each piece, having first line 3 inches from lower edge and others 2¼ inches apart. With three strands of blue floss, embroider yellow rickrack along top line of one section (see stitch detail) to within 10 inches of one end, where the two sections will overlap. With three strands of yellow floss, embroider the green rickrack along the next line in the same way; with three strands of orange floss, embroider the blue rickrack on third line. When putting rickrack on other section of poncho, embroider it to within 10 inches of opposite end. Overlap ends of poncho, covering the ends without rickrack. Sew moss fringe around the bottom, then cover top of fringe with another row of yellow rickrack and blue floss.

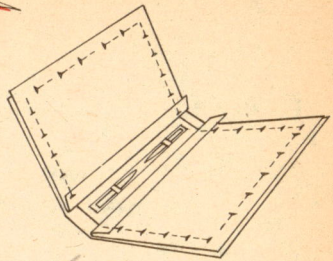

Boutique Portfolio

You need:

1/2 yard satin, brocade, or other handsome material, 45 inches wide

Matching thread

Manuscript cover (stiff cardboard), 9 by 11½ inches

1¾ yards gold braid or gimp

Blotting paper

1 yard satin or velvet ribbon

Cut two pieces of fabric 20 inches wide and 1² inches long. Unfasten prongs of manuscript cover and refasten the two sections so that joining overlaps. Place the two pieces of fabric, wrong side out, around cardboard cover, one on the outside and the other on the inside, and pin edges together. Close cover to make sure outside piece will reach around it when it is closed. When fabric fits smoothly, slit *inside* piece down the center of manuscript cover and turn back the raw edges on each side (diagram). Pin in place. Remove manuscript cover by bending the two halves backward, and stitch (or sew) edges of fabric where they are pinned. Snip off the corners beyond the stitching to avoid extra thickness. Turn cover right side out. Sew braid all around the outside edge. Cut ribbon in half. Sew a piece to each side of cover for ties. Insert cardboard cover again, cut a piece of blotting paper 10½ by 18 inches, punch holes on exact center to correspond with holes on metal fastener, and put in blotting paper.

Cover for Portable Typewriter

You need:

> 5/8 yard firmly woven material, preferably uphol-
> stery fabric
>
> Matching thread
>
> 1¼ yards piping, moss fringe, or welting
>
> 4 yards seam binding
>
> 1 yard round or narrow elastic

Make a paper pattern as shown on diagram 1. Center section is 13 inches wide and 20½ inches long. Side sections are
12 inches wide and 5½ inches high. On each side section draw
a diagonal line (dotted line on diagram), starting 1½ inches
from bottom and ending 5 inches from top corner; line will be
6 inches long. Cut off corner on this line. Notch both sides of
center section: notch A, 1½ inches from front edge; notch B,
7½ inches from front edge; notch C, 5½ inches from back edge.
Make notches directly opposite one another on a straight line.

Place pattern on wrong side of fabric, on straight of goods.
Pin in place. If there is a design, center it on center section,
with bottom of design at front edge. Draw outline of patterns
on fabric for stitching lines. Now draw outlines for cutting,
allowing 1 inch for hem at back and front of center section
and bottom edge of side sections. Allow exactly 1/2 inch on
other edges for seams. Cut out fabric on cutting lines, and
make notches on seam allowance to correspond with those
on paper pattern.

Piping or moss fringe is sewed to right side of notched edges
(diagram 2). The part of piping or fringe that will be hidden
in the seam faces raw edge of fabric. Be sure to stitch on
stitching line.

48

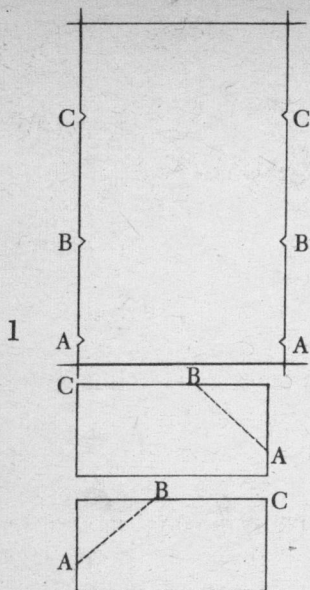

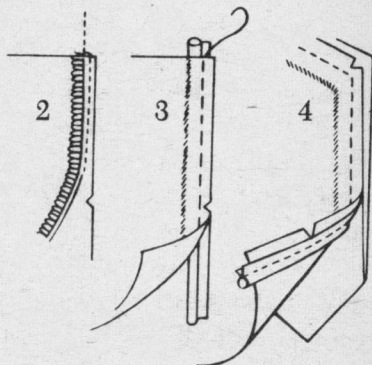

To attach welting by sewing machine, you will need a cording foot. Welting goes on the machine with corded part at left. Place one notched edge, wrong side up, over cording, with raw edge at right (diagram 3). You can see the stitching line and feel the cording through the fabric. Hold welting against stitching line as you sew.

Now pin and sew side sections to center section as follows: Pin edges with right sides together, matching corners A, B, and C to corresponding notches. Place on sewing machine with center section on top, so you can see stitching line (diagram 4). Keeping edges even, stitch over previous stitching line. Check seams on the right side to make sure they are nice and even. Now stitch seam binding over raw edge at bottom. Make 1-inch hem, leaving small opening at back. Run elastic through hem and sew ends of elastic securely together. Sew opening. Cover seam edges with seam binding. Seams and hems may need pressing.

To make a typewriter cover for a man, use felt or leatherette, ticking, or any heavy masculine material. You will need a special needle for sewing leatherette by machine.

More Ideas. Using a pretty printed fabric — such as calico, checked gingham, Toile de Jouy, cretonne, or chintz — you can make covers for stacks of plates, toasters, mixers, electric can openers, electric fans, and other household appliances. These covers should be large enough to slip on and off easily. Keep the shapes as simple as possible. Make your own patterns by cutting and pinning some old material or unbleached muslin until you have sections the right size. Baste these sections together carefully, trim the seams to measure 1/2 inch; then notch the seams (use one, two, or three notches so that they can be identified easily). Rip the pieces apart and make paper patterns that will be easier to work from. A simple way to assemble these covers is to stitch the seams on the right side, then bind the seams and edges with bias binding in a matching or contrasting color.

Baby's Bib

You need:
Bright-colored washcloth
1 package each of rickrack (regular size) and bias binding
Black and green embroidery floss

Twist two lengths of rickrack together, locking points. Turning under raw ends, pin sections of rickrack to form bodies of cats. "Walking Cat" is made with an arch of rickrack 7 inches long, curved so that the ends are 2½ inches apart. A curve of rickrack 5 inches long forms lower edge of body and other two legs. Pin these pieces firmly in place. For head, twist rickrack in a circle until it is about the size of a quarter, then

leave 1/2-inch end for neck and tuck end of neck under body. Pin in place. For ears, cut three points of single rickrack, fold to form a triangle, and pin one to each side of head with raw edges hidden underneath. For tail, use a 3-inch length of single rickrack. Baste all pieces securely, then stitch around all edges. Make a circle of stitching around center of head to form cat's muzzle. With three strands of embroidery floss, embroider a triangle for nose, green circles with black pupils for eyes, and whiskers.

"Sitting Cat" is made with a piece of twisted rickrack 9 inches long. Measure off 1½ inches for front paw, then form remainder into a loop for body. Tail is a 3-inch length of twisted rickrack; head and ears are the same as for "Walking Cat."

To cut out neck of bib, make a pencil mark 1½ inches directly below center of top edge on washcloth. Place the edge of a saucer over top of bib, just touching pencil mark. Draw curve of saucer, and cut out along this line. Leaving 12-inch ends for ties, bind neck edge with bias binding; then sew folded edges of ties together.

Child's Smock (1 to 2 years)

You need:

1/2 yard percale or similar fabric

1 package bias binding in a contrasting color

2 packages rickrack (regular size): one to match bias binding, the other in a different contrasting color

2 skeins embroidery floss to match colors of rickrack

Make paper pattern as shown in diagram. Cut paper 11 by 16 inches. Make a pencil mark at A, 2 inches from one short edge. Make another mark at B, 5 inches from dotted line on other short edge. Draw a diagonal line from A to B, then draw a curve from A to dotted line for bottom curve of smock. For neck, make a mark at C (1½ inches from B), and a mark at D (2½ inches below top). Put a 6-inch saucer over the corner between C and D, and draw a curve along edge of saucer. Slant shoulder down slightly, then use a 7-inch plate to draw the armhole curve from shoulder to E (10½ inches above lower edge).

When cutting front, place dotted line of pattern on lengthwise fold of fabric and allow 1/2 inch for shoulder and side seams. When cutting back, dotted line can go on a selvage edge; allow 1/2 inch for shoulder and side seams and use the 7-inch plate to curve lower edge.

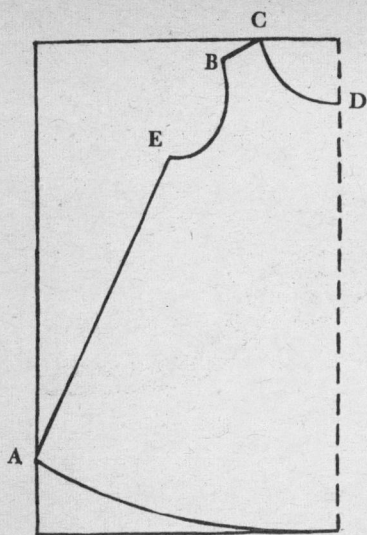

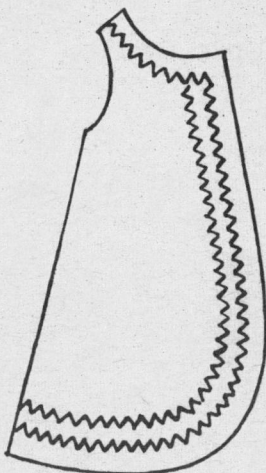

Sew shoulders and sides together with French seams: stitch them first right side out, 1/8 inch from edge. Turn wrong side out, creasing the first seams on stitching lines; then stitch 3/8 inch from first stitching lines. Press seams. Bind all edges with bias binding. Embroider two rows with different colors of rickrack (see page 44) around back and lower edges, using three strands of the opposite color floss for each row. Embroider one row around neck. Close back of neck with hook and eye.

More Ideas. Make little girls' aprons, blouses, or dresses from commercial patterns. Trim with rickrack, colorful braid, or embroidery.

Wedding-dress Hanger

You need:
>Wooden coat hanger covered with white fabric
>1 yard gold and white ribbon, 1 inch wide
>2 yards lace edging

Cut one piece of ribbon 2 inches longer than width of hanger. Turn under 1/2 inch at each end and sew lace around all edges. Sew this piece to one side of hanger; then sew plain ribbon on opposite side, turning under raw ends.

More Ideas. Cover a hanger with white velvet. Tie a satin bow at base of hook and add a bunch of artificial lilies of the valley or a small sachet.

Party-dress Hanger

You need:
>Fabric-covered coat hanger
>1 yard brocaded ribbon, 1¼ inches wide
>1/2 yard narrow velvet ribbon
>2 heavy snap fasteners

Cover both sides of coat hanger with brocaded ribbon. Cut two lengths of velvet ribbon 1 inch longer than side of hanger. Hem both ends. Sew one end to hanger next to hook; fasten

54

other end with snap fastener. Sew other length to opposite side in the same manner. The velvet ribbons can be fastened over the shoulder straps of a party dress.

More Ideas. Cover coat hangers with fake fur, plush, velveteen, or satin.

Christmas Stocking

You need:
>1/2 yard white felt
>Red and green sequins with tiny matching crystal beads
>Star sequins
>Rhinestones and pearl beads
>Gold fringe, braid, and cord

Make a paper stocking pattern — about 14 inches long, 7 inches wide at the top, 5½ inches wide at the ankle, and 8 inches from heel to toe. Foot should tilt down slightly at toe; leg should curve out at calf and heel. Cut two pieces of felt from pattern.

Make a drawing of each decoration you want to embroider. These can include a Christmas tree or tree ornaments; sprays of holly and mistletoe; a wreath, bell, star, or garland; even a gift package tied with red ribbon, or just a big red ribbon bow.

Put drawings on the shiny side of carbon paper and go over the lines, transferring carbon to wrong side of drawing. Place each drawing on front section of stocking and go over the lines again, this time transferring carbon from back of drawing to felt.

Sew sequins to outlines; each sequin is held in place with a crystal bead. Use pearls for mistletoe berries; trim ball ornament with gold braid and rhinestones. Use red sequins for holly berries and for trimmings on Christmas tree. Scatter star sequins among the other trimmings.

Stitch a row of gold fringe across top of this piece. Pin the two felt sections together and baste gold braid around other edges. Stitch the sections together through all three thicknesses. Sew a loop of gold cord to top back corner.

More Ideas. Make a mammoth stocking to hang on the front door; fill it with paper and top it with empty boxes wrapped in foil to resemble gifts. Make stockings of red or green felt, and trim the tops with white plush or ball fringe. Use a real stocking — preferably cotton and inexpensive — and sew felt shoes or high-heeled slippers to the feet, with a lace garter around the top.

Knitting Bag

You need:
> 1/2 yard heavy material, if it can be used sideways,
> 2/3 yard if it has to be used lengthwise
> Piece of felt 24 inches square for lining
> Matching thread
> Bag handles

Cut a piece of material 18 by 24 inches. Cut felt same size. Fold material in half to measure 18 inches wide and 12 inches long. Curve corners of folded edge slightly for bottom of bag. Starting 7 inches from bottom fold, curve top corners gently toward top. Fold and cut felt the same way. With right sides together, stitch sides of bag from bottom fold to start of upper curves. From remaining felt, cut a piece 6 by 14 inches for pocket. Fold this piece in half so that it will measure 6 by 7 inches; folded edge will be top of pocket. Pin pocket on center of felt lining, with folded edge 3 inches from one top edge. Stitch other three sides in place. Fold lining in half again, with pocket on the inside, and stitch sides from bottom fold to start of upper curves. Turn bag right side out and insert lining. Turning under raw edges, sew lining to bag along upper curves to within 1½ inches of top edge. Trimming away 1 inch of felt, pin top edges of bag over the bars of bag handles, gathering extra fullness into a pleat on each side. Hem top edges to lining.

Embroidery Stitches

Chain Stitch. Chain stitch may be used to form an outline, or worked in rounds to fill an area. If it is worked in rounds, start at outer edge and work toward center. Holding yarn or thread under tip of needle, bring up needle on outline about 1/4 to 1/2 inch beyond where it was inserted. Insert needle close to where it was brought up to make next stitch; each stitch locks the loop of previous stitch in place. Secure the loop of last stitch by inserting needle through to wrong side over tip of loop.

Feather Stitching. Starting at top left, bring needle to right side. Holding yarn or thread under tip of needle, take a small downward stitch 1/2 inch diagonally on the right. Always holding yarn or thread under needle tip, take a downward stitch directly under the left-hand stitch, take a downward stitch directly under the right-hand stitch. Repeat for desired length. Insert needle to wrong side over last loop made.

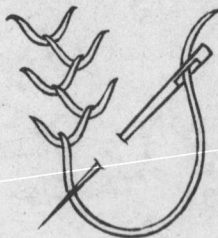

Fly Stitch. Bring up needle to right side. Insert needle 1/2 inch to the right; holding yarn or thread under tip of needle, bring up needle 1/2 inch down and halfway between where needle was brought up and where it was inserted. Insert needle to wrong side below the loop thus formed.

French Knot. Bring up needle to right side and take a very small stitch in the same place, leaving needle only half drawn through fabric. Wrap yarn or thread nearest the fabric, two or three times over tip of needle. Holding these loops against fabric, draw needle through, then insert it in the same place where it was brought up.

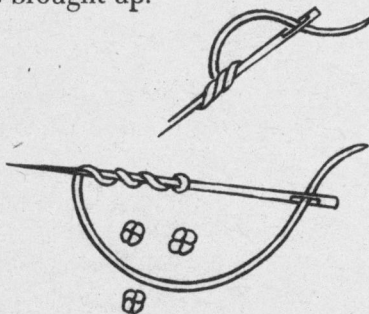

Lazy Daisy Stitch. This stitch is worked the same as one single chain stitch, then secured in place by inserting the needle to wrong side over tip of loop.

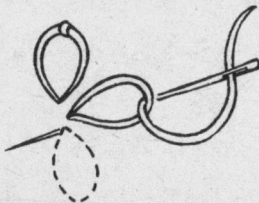

Outline, Stem, or Back Stitch. Work along an outline. Bring up needle to right side at one end of the line to be embroidered. Insert needle on same line, about 3/8 inch beyond where it was brought up and return it about halfway back, then draw it through. Continue inserting needle 3/8 inch further along line and bringing it up halfway back, forming a narrow row of stitches. When turning a curve, bring up needle on the *inner* side, so that previous stitch will be held against the *outer* side of curve.

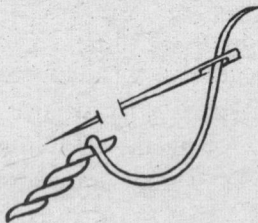

Blanket Stitch. Bring up needle desired distance from edge; holding yarn under tip of needle, insert at same distance from edge and bring up at edge.

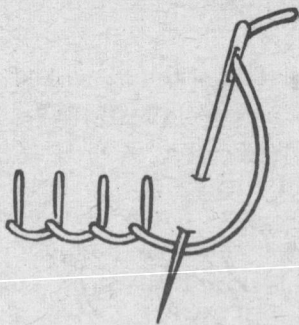

Tassels

Cut a piece of cardboard about 1/2 inch longer than desired finished length of tassel. Wrap cardboard with yarn until tassel is desired thickness. Slip a separate strand of yarn under these strands at one end of cardboard and tie tightly; ends of this strand will be used for attaching tassel. Cut strands at opposite end of cardboard. With another strand of yarn, wrap top of tassel for about one fifth of its length; fasten ends of this strand by threading them into a rug needle and drawing them into the top of tassel. Even off ends of tassel.

Pompons

If you are making a great many, you can buy plastic pompon makers in various sizes at the needlework store or counter. You can also cut two circles of cardboard about 1/2 inch larger than desired finished size of pompon. Cut a hole the size of a dime in center of each circle. Thread a rug needle with a double strand of yarn 2 yards long. Hold the two circles together and wrap this double cardboard with yarn by inserting needle through hole and around edge, until edges are evenly covered. When yarn is used up, take another length and continue until center hole is packed tight.

Clip yarn around the edge by inserting tip of scissors between the two circles, then pass a double strand of yarn between the two cardboards and tie the strands tightly together; the ends of this double strand will be used for sewing pompon in place. Remove cardboard, shake pompon, then even off ends of strands.

PALETTE and PAINT

BEFORE YOU DECIDE to decorate anything, make sure that you have the proper paints and brushes, or other equipment, for the surface on which you plan to work. Oil paints can be used on stone, wood, earthenware, metal, or straw; water colors on paper; fabric paint on cloth; china paint on china — this also requires access to a kiln. Crayons can be used on felt; so can cutouts of iron-on tape. You can even "paint" with iron-on tape: cut snippets of various colors with scissors or a punch, then overlap these bits to shade into new color effects. Try this method for "painting" flowers on a dish towel or place mat. It's unusual, inexpensive, and a lot of fun!

Start by making sketches of your design; then make a finished drawing and color it with crayons or water colors. It is easier to make corrections on your drawing than on the surface you plan to decorate. Unless you are an accomplished artist, let original ideas compensate for any lack of skill: do stylized animals, tell an amusing story with stick figures, or use simple decorative designs. Trace or copy patterns, but be sure to make a few changes that will turn any copies into your own, personal creation.

If you find something you would like to trace, but that needs to be enlarged, find out how much it would cost to have a photostat enlargement made. The classified section of the telephone book will help you find the names of photographers who make photostats.

When you have made a satisfactory drawing, transfer the outlines with carbon paper. If the surface is hard, such as glass

62

or metal, fasten the carbon paper in place, carbon side down, with cellophane tape or masking tape. Then fasten the drawing on top of the carbon paper and go over the outlines with a hard pencil. If the surface is soft, such as paper or fabric, put your drawing on top of the shiny side of the carbon paper and go over the outlines, transferring the carbon from the carbon paper to the wrong side of the drawing. Then fasten the drawing in place and go over the lines again, this time transferring the carbon from the back of the drawing. This method will eliminate smudges.

Oil paints take a long time to dry. After they have set, they should be given a coat of spray varnish to protect them. This is especially important for anything that will be subjected to wear or water, such as glass and metal.

Painted Tray

You need:
    Inexpensive tray
    Flat paint and paint brush
    Oil paints and brushes, or decorative pictures
      and glue
    Masking tape
    Spray varnish

Paint tray with flat paint — glossy enamel does not hold oil paints easily. For a painted design, draw your design on paper, make stencils (see page 65), or plan to paint the design freehand after transferring outlines to tray. The center of the tray can be divided into sections, with painted frames to hold several pictures or small paintings. Use masking tape to keep the lines of the frames straight. For a painted design, fill in the outlines carefully. Set the tray in a warm place, where it will be protected from dust until it is thoroughly dry. Spray with varnish.

If you are going to decorate it with pictures, you can find something interesting by sending away for decorative maps, reprints "suitable for framing" from magazines, or by rummaging for bargains in second-hand bookstores where there may be some damaged books or periodicals with old-fashioned pictures. Remember, you don't have to have one picture to fill the center of the tray; often a grouping of several small pictures will make an interesting effect. They can overlap or be put in separate painted frames. Spray with varnish.

More Ideas. Decorate canisters, wooden or metal boxes, lunchboxes, tin cans for holding various items. Paint designs on inexpensive straw hats, place mats, or tote bags.

Stenciled Place Mat

You need:
Butcher linen
Textile paints
Paint mixer
Stencil brush
3 or 4 pieces of stencil paper, one for each color
Stencil knife
Blotting paper
Cellophane tape
Heavy cardboard or oaktag

Cut linen to desired size for place mat. Fringe or hem edges. Wash, rinse, and press, to remove any sizing in fabric.

Make or trace a drawing for your design and color it with crayons or water colors, using only three or four flat colors. Outline each color section with ink.

Fasten a piece of stencil paper over the drawing with cellophane tape. Mark position of stencil paper on drawing so that each stencil will be placed in exactly the same position. Trace the outlines of the lightest color. Mark this stencil No. 1. Place another stencil paper over drawing in the same position and trace outlines of next lightest color. Mark this stencil No. 2. Continue tracing outlines of each color on a separate stencil, from lightest to darkest, numbering each stencil.

Put the stencils on heavy cardboard or oaktag, and cut around outlines with stencil knife. Tack blotting paper to a board; then tack linen on top of blotter, stretching it evenly and firmly. Tack stencil No. 1 in position on the linen and mark the corners so that the "register" (proper placement of all the colors to match drawing) will be exactly right.

Measure about a teaspoonful of mixer on a saucer. Add a small amount of the color you want for the lightest shade. You can mix in bits of another color to get the tone you prefer, then add white for lightening or black for darkening it. Get

the color just right before you begin to paint; try it out on a sample of cloth. Dip in the brush; then wipe off excess paint on edge of saucer. If there is too much paint on the brush, it may creep under edges of stencil. Apply paint to openings in stencil: hold brush straight up and down, and use a circular motion. When all segments for this stencil have been painted, remove stencil. If you are painting several place mats, paint the same color on all of them first.

Clean brush, mix next color on a fresh saucer, and place second stencil in the same position. Continue in this way until all colors have been painted in. Let the painted linen dry overnight.

The paint is "set" with an iron. Take care not to scorch the linen. Set iron for "Linen" and press painted sections from the wrong side for a total of about three minutes. If linen gets too hot and scorching might occur, press for a moment, let the linen cool, then press again. Turn linen right side up and repeat the process, this time working through a dry cloth.

More Ideas. Stencil designs on T shirts, dish towels, aprons, silk scarves (on silk, use a warm iron and press for a longer time), crib sheets, baby pillow cases. Stencils can also be used on other materials, such as metal or wood, with oil paints or house paints. Fabric paints can be used for freehand painting; they need to be thinned slightly with a paint thinner and applied with a camel's-hair brush. Always work with a blotter under the fabric to absorb extra paint and keep it from spreading.

66

Painted Apothecary Jar

You need:
Apothecary jar
Oil paints or gold paint
Water-color brush
Spray varnish

You can either work freehand, or transfer a drawing or tracing to the glass as a guide. Instead of the usual rosebuds, forget-me-nots, or daisies, paint a Japanese willow tree, a delicate branch of apple blossoms, or ferns.

Paint the design on one side of the jar, on the front and back, or on all four sides. Paint a little design on the stopper and around the top and neck of the jar. Let the paint dry for several days in a warm, dry place; then spray with varnish.

The jar illustrated was painted with oil paints to resemble gold leaf: yellow paint was mixed with a touch each of brown and of black; but the colors were not blended, so that tones would vary slightly as they were applied.

These jars are perfect containers for cotton balls, hair-set lotion, cotton swabs, hair curlers, and dozens of other things. They can also be decorated suitably for the kitchen and used for tea bags, spices, toothpicks, matches, and innumerable other kitchen supplies.

More Ideas. Decorate bottles, decanters, glasses, coasters, trivets, glass or plastic containers of any kind.

Painted Light-switch Plate

You need:
Light-switch plate
Oil paints
Water-color brush
Decals, or other decorations and glue
Spray varnish

Paint a garland of tiny flowers on the light-switch plate.
You can also add a decal of a cupid and a few tiny artificial
flowers. Spray completed plate with varnish when paint is
dry. The decorations should not be placed too close to the
opening where they would interfere with the light switch.

More Ideas. Paint the flat frames of bolts and chain bolts,
cupboard hinges, or other hardware. Decorate china door-
knobs with china paint.

Painted Wastebasket

You need:
Metal wastebasket
Flat black paint and paint brush
Gold paint and small striping brush
Oil paints, brushes, and white carbon paper;
  or decorative picture and glue
Spray varnish
Masking tape

Paint wastebasket black. After the paint is dry, draw an outline for the picture with pencil and ruler. Put masking tape about 1/4 inch outside of the pencil lines. With gold paint, make a frame for the picture inside the masking tape. Remove tape. Using masking tape to keep lines straight, paint gold trim on top and bottom edges of basket.

Glue the decorative picture inside the frame, or make a drawing of what you want to paint and transfer it to basket (as explained on page 62). Use oil paints for painting this picture. When all the paint or glue is thoroughly dry, spray entire basket with varnish.

KNICKNACKS
for KNITTERS

How would you like to knit yourself a smart pony-tail cap, or crochet a pair of amusing slippers for your best beau?

If you don't know how to knit or crochet, you can buy a "learn-how" book at the chain or variety store.

A hand-knitted sweater for your mother, or a pair of Argyle socks for the man in your life, would be super gifts. Instructions for these can be found in knitting books and needlework magazines, so they are not included here. Instead, all the items in this chapter are things you can whip up in an evening or two — depending on how much homework you have and how quickly you get it done — and any one of them might be turned into a profitable venture.

The Most Important Thing

Everything you knit or crochet is planned for a certain size, and for a certain amount of yarn or thread. Each set of instructions carries a *gauge*. This is the number of stitches that should make one inch. The number of rows per inch may also be included.

If your stitches are looser than they should be, the finished piece will come out larger and take more yarn; if you work more tightly than you are supposed to, of course the finished piece will be too small. Even experienced knitters (who should know better) may go blithely along without checking the gauge, then express astonishment if the sweater, mittens or socks don't fit! One customer complained bitterly to the manufacturer that he hadn't recommended enough yarn to finish the sleeves of a pullover. When she sent in her work, it turned out that the back and front each measured 26 inches wide instead of 17 inches. Of course, she didn't have enough yarn to finish the sleeves, and if she had completed the pullover, it would have been a size 52 instead of a size 12!

So *always* make a sample piece before you begin. (Even a different color of the same yarn can make a difference in the gauge!) If your sample turns out too big, change to smaller needles or crochet hook; if it comes out too small, change to larger needles or crochet hook. Only when your sample measures the right size are you ready to start work.

The Professional Look

Ripping. When you make a mistake — and everybody does occasionally — *rip!* Do it right away, before you have time to argue yourself into believing that "nobody will ever notice it."

Here are some helpful hints:

If you have to rip knitting, rip back to the row just above the mistake. Now rip the offending row, a stitch at a time; as each stitch is released, insert the needle into it. This is easier to do with a smaller needle. Be careful not to twist the stitches.

If you have to rip crochet, be sure to count the rows as you rip, so that you know exactly where to start again.

Picking Up a Dropped Stitch. If you drop a stitch, and notice it *before any rows have closed in over it,* you can pick it up easily on the knit side with a crochet hook: slip the hook through the dropped stitch, from front to back, draw the strand above it through the dropped stitch, then draw the strand of the row above through this stitch. This can be done all the way to the top.

Blocking. Separate pieces should be blocked before they

71

are sewed together. Pin them to the proper size on an ironing board, using a ruler to check measurements. Cover them with a damp cloth and use the iron to steam the moisture through the knitting.

Washing. If your work is soiled, wash it in lukewarm suds, squeezing the suds through the yarn; never wring or rub the wool. *Always support the weight of the yarn while it is wet, to keep it from stretching.* Lift the clean, rinsed garment and use a turkish towel to press out excess water. Synthetic yarns must be dried on a smooth towel, so they can creep back to size; woolen yarn should be patted into shape and dried on a turkish towel.

Sewing. Use matching yarn if you can. If the yarn is too bulky or nubby for sewing, use matching thread. An invisible seam can be made with yarn by working on the right side and taking a stitch alternately in one edge, then in the other. This joins each row to the corresponding row. When rows don't match exactly, pin the edges together on the wrong side; then sew the seam with running stitches and an occasional backstitch, close to the edge. Overcasting should be done only when joining ribbing, and of course only on the wrong side. Catch together one stitch on each edge. Seams can be steamed lightly.

Abbreviations and Terms

beg: beginning
ch: chain
dc: double crochet
dec: decrease
inc: increase
k: knit

p: purl
pr: pair
psso: pass slipped stitch over
rnd: round
sc: single crochet

sl: slip
sl st: crocheted slip stitch
st: stitch
sts: stitches
tog: together

* : Repeat whatever follows the asterisk as many times as specified.
Stockinette stitch: K 1 row, p 1 row. Knit side is right side.
Garter stitch: K every row; 2 rows make 1 ridge.

Pony-tail Cap

You need:

    Knitting worsted: 1 ounce main color,
        1/3 ounce contrasting color
    1 pair No. 6 knitting needles
    Size G crochet hook
    Gauge: 5 sts = 1 inch; 7 rows = 1 inch

Sample Piece: To check your gauge, cast on 15 sts and work in stockinette stitch for 21 rows. This should make a 3-inch square.

Cap (make 2 pieces the same): Starting at outer edge with main color cast on 52 sts. K 1 row, p 1 row, k 2 rows. *Row 5:* K 2 tog; k to last 2 sts; inserting needle through *back* of sts, k 2 tog. *Row 6:* Purl. Repeat rows 5 and 6 until 30 sts remain. Bind off.

Finishing: Pin pieces right sides together to hold them flat; press through a damp cloth. Sew side seams. Hold cap with right side toward you and, using contrasting color, work 1 row of single crochet *loosely* in every other st around both edges.

Cords and Pompons: Attach contrasting color yarn to seam at corner of cap; make a chain 10 inches long. Slip stitch in 2nd chain from hook and each chain. Fasten off. Make pompon with contrasting color (see page 61), and fasten to end of cord.

Crocheted
Cleanser Cover

You need:
  2 balls heavy weight speed crochet cotton thread
  No. 1 steel crochet hook
  Can of cleanser
  1/4 yard each of two colors velvet ribbon
  Small spray of artificial flowers
  Gauge: 5 sts = 1 inch; 2 rows = 1 inch

Starting at bottom of cover, wrap thread over one finger to form a ring. Insert hook in this ring and draw thread through, ch 1. *Rnd 1:* Make 8 sc in ring. Pull up end of thread to tighten ring. *Rnd 2:* Working over end of thread, make 2 sc in each sc around (16 sc). Mark beg of rnds, but do not join rnds. *Rnd 3:* * 2 sc in next sc, 1 sc in next sc. Repeat from * around (24 sc). *Rnd 4:* * 2 sc in next sc, 1 sc in each of the next 2 sc. Repeat from * around (32 sc). *Rnd 5:* * 2 sc in next sc, 1 sc in each of the next 3 sc. Repeat from * around (40 sc). *Rnd 6:* * 2 sc in next sc, 1 sc in each of the next 4 sc. Repeat from * around (48 sc). Now work 1 sc in each sc around for 1 or 2 rnds, until piece measures same as bottom of can.

Shape Sides: Rnd 1: Sc in back loop of each sc around. *Rnd 2:* * Sc in next sc, skip 1 sc, make 3 dc in next sc, skip next sc. Repeat from * around. *Rnd 3:* * 3 dc in next sc, sc in center dc of 3-dc group. Repeat from * around. Repeat Rnd 3 until piece will reach to top of can. *Next rnd:* Sc in each st around.

Last rnd: * Pull up a loop in each of the next 2 sc, draw thread through all 3 loops on hook (1 sc decreased), sc in next 4 sc. Repeat from * around. Slip st in next 3 or 4 sts. Break thread and fasten off. Trim cover with ribbons, looped at center, and flower spray. Insert cleanser can.

More Ideas. Make a set of glass jackets. Use a glass for measuring bottom circle, and stop increases when circle is about 1/2 inch smaller than bottom of glass. Omit last rnd of cleanser cover. Make a cover for a bottle or pitcher with straight sides; continue to inc 8 sc on each rnd until bottom circle is 1/2 inch smaller than bottom of bottle or pitcher.

Fido Feet

Sizes: Small (Medium-Large)

You need:

Knitting worsted: 2 ounces beige, 1 ounce brown, scraps of black

1 pair No. 2 knitting needles

No. 1 steel crochet hook

1 pair inner soles (size 6-6½, small; 7-7½, medium; 8-8½, large)

Cardboard

1/4 yard brown felt

3/4 yard round elastic

Scraps of black and white felt or 4 "moving eyes"

Gauge: 6 sts = 1 inch; 9 rows = 1 inch

Sample Piece: To check your gauge, cast on 18 sts. Work in stockinette st for 27 rows. Piece should measure 3 inches square.

Slippers: Starting at toe with beige, cast on 10 sts. Work in stockinette st, increasing 1 st at both ends of every k row 7 (8-9) times; 24 (26-28) sts. Inc 1 st at both ends of every 4th row 3 times; 30 (32-34) sts. Work even until total length is 4 (4¼-4½) inches.

Shape Sides: Work first 8 (9-10) sts. Turn and work these sts, increasing 1 st at inner edge every 4th row 8 times. There are 16 (17-18) sts. Work even until outer edge measures 1/2 inch less than edge of inner sole from center of toe to center of heel.

Shape Back Edge: At inner edge bind off 4 sts at beg of every other row 3 times, bind off remaining sts. Slip center 14 sts on a holder for instep, attach yarn, and work remaining 8 (9-10) sts of other side to correspond.

Instep: Work the 14 sts from holder, decreasing 1 st at both ends of every other row twice. Dec 1 st at both ends of *every* row twice. Bind off remaining 6 sts.

Ears: Starting at lower edge with brown, cast on 4 sts. Work in garter st, increasing 1 at both ends of every other row twice. Work even on 8 sts until total length is 2¼ inches. K 2 tog across each of the next 2 rows: 2 sts remain. K 2 tog. Break yarn and draw end through last st.

Finishing: Cut 4 pieces of cardboard same size as inner soles and 4 pieces of felt slightly larger. Place 2 pieces of cardboard on each inner sole and cover with felt, overcasting edges together. Sew back seams; then sew slipper to soles. With brown, work 1 row single crochet across instep; then working over elastic, continue single crochet around remaining top edge of slipper. Sew one end of elastic in place, draw up to fit snugly, sew other end. Embroider nose with black, making 3 long sts, then weaving in and out of these sts as shown on diagram. Sew on ears. For eyes, cut out black and white felt and sew in place, as shown on diagram, or sew on "moving eyes."

More Ideas. Make plain slippers, and trim them with pompons or velvet bows, flowers, or sequins. Use white or gray yarn, and turn them into pussy cats by embroidering a heart-shaped nose, whiskers, and an inverted V for mouth; use large green sequins on a piece of black felt for eyes. Use white yarn and turn them into bunny rabbits by embroidering nose and eyes with pink, adding white whiskers (use pipe cleaners) and white felt ears lined with pink. Turn them into little raccoons by cutting masks of black felt and making round bead eyes. Sew long strands of yarn together down the center and sew these across the toe, trimming off the ends to touch sole edges; then use "moving eyes" or black button eyes, turning the slippers into little Maltese terriers.

Wooly Lamb Slippers

(These crocheted slippers will fit any foot from size 6 to 9.)

You need:
4 ounces knitting worsted
Size G crochet hook
3/4 yard of 2-inch ribbon or other trimming
5/8 yard round elastic
Gauge: 4 sts = 1 inch; 4 rows = 1 inch

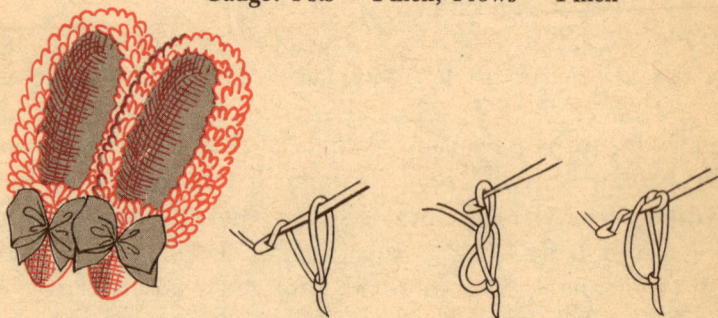

Starting at toe, ch 2. *Rnd 1:* Make 5 sc in 2nd ch from hook. Do not join rnds, but mark beg of every rnd for accurate shaping. *Rnd 2:* 2 sc in each sc around (10 sc). *Rnd 3:* * 2 sc in next sc, 1 sc in next sc. Repeat from * around (15 sc). *Rnd 4:* * 2 sc in next sc, 1 sc in each of the next 2 sc. Repeat from * around (20 sc). *Rnd 5:* * 2 sc in next sc, 1 sc in each of the next 3 sc. Repeat from * around (25 sc). *Rnd 6:* * 2 sc in next sc, 1 sc in each of the next 4 sc. Repeat from * around (30 sc). *Rnds 7-13:* 1 sc in each sc around. *Rnds 14 and 15:* 1 sc in *back loop* only of each sc around.

Shape Sides: Row 1 (wrong side): Ch 1, turn; sc in first 24 sc. *Row 2:* Ch 1, turn, sc in *back loop* only of first 24 sc. *Rows 3-20:* Repeat these 2 rows, then repeat Row 1 once more.

Shape Heel: Row 22 (right side): Ch 1, turn; working in back loops, sc in 10 sc, pull up a loop in each of the next 2 sc, draw yarn through all 3 loops on hook *(1 sc decreased);* dec 1

78

sc over the next 2 sc, sc in remaining 10 sc. *Row 23:* Ch 1, turn; sc in 9 sc, dec 1 sc twice, sc in 9 sc. *Row 24:* Ch 1, turn, working in back loops, sc in 8 sc, dec 1 sc twice, sc in 8 sc.

Loops: Draw up loop on hook to measure 3/4 inch. Draw yarn through this long loop; inserting hook between the long loop and the single strand beside it (see diagram), make an sc. This completes 1 knot st. Turn work around so that you can work across the free loops below last row, * sc in first free loop, make a knot st. Repeat from * across. Work across next row of free loops in same way. Now work rows of knot sts and sc across the first 8 free loops along one side to instep. Break off and fasten. Skip 8 sts for sole, attach yarn in next free loop on opposite side and work knot st loops on the 8 free loops of other side edge. Skipping the 8 sts of sole, work 2 rows of knot st loops across all other free loops below instep. Fasten off. Sew back seam. Run elastic through sts around top edge. Draw up elastic to fit snugly, cut off extra length and fasten ends securely. Cut ribbon in half, run a row of gathering sts across center and pull tight; then gather each side, halfway between center and end. Bring gathered parts together to form a bow, sew tightly together and sew to front of slipper.

More Ideas. Trim slipper with a big pompon. Embroider a puppy-dog nose and add eyes (see page 77). Trim with one big flower or a small bunch of flowers. Instead of running elastic through the top, use narrow ribbon and tie the ends in a bow at the front. Sew sequins and other fake jewels across the top of the toe. Work *all* the sc in back loops, and cover the entire toe with knot st loops. Use two colors of yarn: one for the sc, the other for the knot st loops.

To make slippers for a man, use a masculine color (black, brown, gray, maroon, navy), work one extra increase rnd (35 sc). For the sides, work first 28 sts and work for 26 rows before shaping heel. Work loops on 9 sts on each side, skipping 10 sts for sole. Do not add any trimming.

Crocheted potholder

You need:
2 70-yard skeins rug yarn
Size G crochet hook
Brass curtain ring
Gauge: 3 sts = 1 inch; 3 rows = 1 inch

Chain 20 sts to measure about 7 inches. *Row 1:* Sc in second ch from hook and each ch across. *Row 2:* Ch 1, turn, sc in each sc across. Repeat Row 2 until piece is square. Break yarn and fasten off. Make another piece exactly the same. Whip edges together. Sew ring to one corner.

More Ideas. Crochet raffia squares for place mats. Crochet squares in interesting color combinations for pillow covers, tote bags, or stoles.

Knitted Potholder

You need:
1 skein (70 yards) rug yarn
1 pair No. 8 knitting needles
Brass curtain ring
Gauge: 4 sts = 1 inch; 8 rows = 1 inch

Cast on 28 sts. K every row until piece is square. Bind off. Make another piece exactly the same. Whip edges together (insert padding if desired). Sew ring to one corner. If you make these of pretty colors, suitable for a kitchen, they are gay, useful gifts — and are saleable, too.

More Ideas. Make knitted squares about 4 inches wide in several colors of baby yarn sew them together for a baby's blanket or carriage robe. Knit squares of bright yarn and join them to make lap robes, afghans, ponchos — even a sleeveless slip-on sweater.

POTPOURRI

Potpourri (pronounced *poh-poor-ree*) has two meanings: it can refer to a fragrant mixture of dried flower petals or to a medley of diversified, unrelated things.

Even if you love dabbling in glue, can paint like a professional artist, sew as well as a French dressmaker, and never drop a stitch when you knit, you may want to make some of the things that are presented in this chapter. They take very little time and skill, but are quite charming, and make delightful gifts.

Pomander —
an old-fashioned sachet

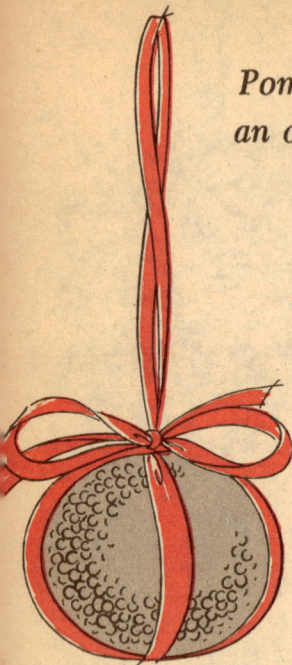

You need:
   Small, firm orange or apple; for miniature
   pomanders, use lady apples, crab apples,
   or kumquats
   1 box of cloves (not previously opened)
   1 teaspoonful ground cinnamon
   1 tablespoonful orrisroot powder
   Medium-sized paper bag
   1 yard narrow velvet ribbon
   Plastic film

Using only cloves with long, pointed stems, insert two rows
around the fruit, dividing it into equal quarters. Continue to
insert cloves, close together, until each quarter is solidly filled.
Put cinnamon and orrisroot powder into paper bag, drop in
pomander, and shake until fruit is coated with the powder.
Keep bag closed and put in a dark, dry, cool place to cure for
several days. (You can use the same bag of powder for coat-
ing several pomanders at the same time.) When the pomander has been cured sufficiently, remove from bag and tie ribbon around it, using pins to hold ribbon if necessary. Wrap
pomander in plastic film to preserve fragrance until ready for
use. Wonderful for linen closets!

Naughty Cat Place Mat

You need:

Piece of solid-color linen or cotton cloth approximately
13 by 18 inches
2 or 3 packages of press-on fabric in contrasting colors
Tracing and carbon paper

Cut place mat from cloth in desired shape and size. Hem, fringe, or bind edges. Draw or trace outline of a cat on tracing paper. (If your cat picture is too small, you can have a photostatic enlargement made. The Yellow Pages of the telephone directory list places that make these.) Put tracing paper on shiny side of carbon paper and go over lines of drawing, transferring carbon outline to back of tracing paper. Pin drawing to press-on fabric and trace again, this time transferring carbon outline to fabric. Cut out design, arrange on place mat, and iron on firmly as directed on package so that it adheres to mat.

More Ideas. Find other designs to trace, or make up your own. Decorate work gloves, fabric hats, and caps from chain or variety store; aprons, T shirts, tote bags, potholders, dishtowels, sneakers, and kerchiefs. Cut out letters of press-on fabric for names, initials, or even slogans.

Twine Holder

You need:

Round can with removable lid, such as a salted-peanut can, or round plastic box with lid
Ball of twine
Spray paint and varnish
Bright-colored cellophane tape, decals, or stickers

Open can, making sure there are no sharp or jagged edges. Punch a hole in center of lid with icepick or nail. Spray can and lid with paint. Trim with tape, decals or stickers, and spray with varnish. Insert ball of twine, threading end of twine through hole in lid. Fasten lid securely with cellophane tape. Lid must be removable in case end of twine slips out of reach, or a replacement is needed.

More Ideas. Decorate metal candy boxes in same way, fill with homemade candy (to give — not to sell). Cans without lids can be sprayed inside and out, decorated and varnished, and used as pencil holders or flower containers. Small round boxes, such as those that hold typewriter ribbon, can be embellished and used for stamps, buttons, or other small items. Spray a container with gold paint, decorate with cupid decals.

Decorated File Box

You need:
  Wooden or metal file box
  Spray paint and varnish
  Decals or stickers
  Index cards to fit box

Spray box evenly with paint. When dry, trim with decals or stickers, then spray with varnish. Fill box with index cards, to be used for lists of addresses, menus, recipes, or other references.

More Ideas. Appropriately decorated file boxes make charming and useful receptacles for sewing or cooking accessories; stamp or coin collections; odds and ends.

Candle-in-a-Glass

You need:
Gracefully shaped goblet or glass
2 or 3 cakes of paraffin (enough to fill glass)
Candle stub (about 1/2 inch shorter than glass)
Wax crayons for coloring
Double boiler
Stickers, gold-paper ornaments, decals, or other
decorations

Measure capacity of glass, using water and a measuring cup. Melt same amount of paraffin (one cake will fill about half a cup). Break cake into small pieces and place in top of double boiler over burner. *Caution:* Never try to melt paraffin over direct heat, and don't forget to put water in bottom of double boiler. Light burner *after* paraffin is in pot and pot is on burner. Turn off heat *before* removing from stove. *Spilled paraffin is a fire hazard.*

Add crayon. If you want shaded colors, melt a small piece of crayon with the paraffin for the lighter-colored part and pour some into glass; then add more crayon for deeper-colored sections. Melt each amount separately and pour into glass in layers. Let each layer cool before pouring in the next. As paraffin cools, it will sink slightly at center.

As soon as you pour just a bit of paraffin into glass, set candle stub in it. Take care that stub remains upright in center and that it doesn't project above top layer of paraffin. If necessary, cut wick so that it doesn't protrude above rim of glass.

Set filled glass aside at room temperature until paraffin cools completely; then place overnight in refrigerator — but not in freezer, or paraffin will crack.

Decorate glass with stickers, gold-paper ornaments, decals, or other trimmings. (For suggestions, see "Glitter and Glue," pages 14-31).

Topiary Tree

You need:

    Small flowerpot with hole in bottom
    Dowel or long pencil
    2 balls of plastic foam
    Artificial flowers
    2 yards narrow velvet ribbon
    Gold spray paint

Spray flowerpot, dowel, and plastic balls with gold paint. Insert dowel through one ball to form base of tree; wedge ball into flowerpot and push dowel into hole at base to hold it firmly. Insert upper part of dowel into other ball to form top of tree. Decorate top with artificial flowers and two ribbon bows with streamers, pinning each bow in place. Tie two bows around base of tree, one on each side.

More Ideas. Trim tree with pastel flowers for Easter or birthdays; with red roses, holly, mistletoe, or other appropriate decorations for Christmas. For a very special occasion, cover entire top with sequins and fake jewels, or little ribbon bows, pinned in place.

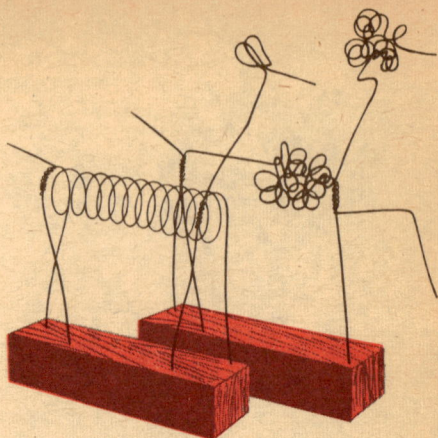

Wire Sculpture

Here is something truly different for you to try. These little figures were designed by William King, a well-known sculptor, whose work is frequently on exhibition in New York.

You need:
>About 12 feet of 24- to 30-gauge wire
>Needle-nosed pliers for bending wire
>Wire cutters
>Pencil and broomstick for wrapping wire spirals
>Wooden bases or plastic foam slabs, about 2 inches
>   wide, 5 inches long, and 3/4 inch thick
>Spray paint

POODLE — Cut a piece of wire about 21 inches long for head and straight front leg. Measure off 1 inch for nose, then wind wire twelve times around pencil. Slide these loops off pencil and twist them into a double circle to form a ball for head. Make a little kink in wire 2 inches below head for base of neck.

Cut a second piece of wire about 32 inches long for raised front leg, body, and one hind leg. Measure off 3½ inches for front leg, then twist together this wire with first wire at base of neck. Using pliers, twist both wires tightly three times so they will be firmly fastened and not slide apart. Remainder of first wire will form front leg; cut this wire to measure 3½ inches below joining.

Wind second piece of wire, beyond joining, around pencil sixteen times for back of poodle. Slide loops off pencil and form them into another ball. Measure off 2½ inches beyond loops and make a little kink in wire.

Cut third piece of wire 6 inches long for tail and hind leg. Measure off 1½ inches for tail, then twist this wire to second wire beyond kink. Bend down both wires above joining to form hind legs and cut them to measure 3½ inches. Bend up the front leg of body wire and bend it down at center. Adjust position of head, neck, tail, and legs to correspond with illustration. Spray figure with paint. Let paint dry.

If you are using a wooden base, place figure on base and mark position of feet; then make small holes in base at marks, using a thin sharp nail. Holes should be 1/4 inch deep. Fill holes with liquid cement or glue and insert feet. If base is plastic foam, wire can be easily inserted.

DEER — Cut a piece of wire 3 feet long for head, body, and tail. Measure off 1⅛ inches for nose, then wind wire twice around pencil. Slide loops off pencil and shape them into ovals opposite one another for ears. Measure off 3 inches for neck and make a little kink in wire for base of neck.

Cut second piece of wire 10 inches long. Using pliers, twist together the center of second wire with the first piece, starting at the kink; twist both wires tightly together four times so that they will be firmly fastened and not slide apart. Bend down both ends of second wire to form front legs.

Wind first wire, beyond joining, nine times around broomstick for body. Slide these loops off broomstick.

Cut third piece of wire 10 inches long. Making sure that joining starts even with *top* of last loop, twist center of third wire to last loop of body wire four times.

Cut body wire 1½ inches beyond joining, for tail. Bend down both ends of third wire to form hind legs. Adjust head, ears, neck, body, legs, and tail to correspond with illustration. Cut legs to measure about 4¼ inches from top of body. Spray figure with paint, let paint dry. Mount figure on base in same way as poodle.

More Ideas. Make flat wire outlines of fish, animals, flowers, fruits, vegetables, or even free forms. Leave a length of wire for mounting them on bases, or attach string for hanging them as mobiles. Glue colored or decorative tissue paper, or other thin, transparent paper, to one side of figure, filling in the space inside wire and cutting off excess beyond the outline.

Kissing Ball

You need:
> Plastic foam ball, about 5 inches in diameter
> 8½ yards olive-green ribbon and 1 yard red ribbon, 1 inch wide
> Artificial mistletoe or olive-green felt and large pearl beads
> Red berries
> Florist's wire
> Green tissue paper or crepe paper
> Glue

Cover ball with strips of green paper, glued smoothly in place. Insert a piece of wire through center of ball. Cut a piece of green ribbon 18 inches long, fasten it to one end of this wire, and tie in a loop for hanging up ball. Attach a bow of red ribbon with long streamers to opposite end of same wire.

Cut remaining ribbon into 12-inch lengths. Fold each piece to form two loops and two ends, then twist a wire around the center to form it into a bow. Insert end of each wire into ball.

Space the bows evenly around ball. Fill in spaces between with leaves and berries, inserting stems directly into ball or using wire to fasten them to plastic foam.

To make your own artificial mistletoe, string two or three pearl beads on a wire, cut out teardrop-shaped leaves from felt, and insert wire through the pointed ends of leaves. Glue tips of leaves to wire to hold them in position.

More Ideas. Cover ball with artificial holly and attach a piece of real or artificial mistletoe to the red bow. Dip a ball in glue, roll it in sequins and glitter, and attach mistletoe.

Christmas Tree

You need:
Small artificial tree
2 strings of little glass ornaments
Beads, large sequins, or other miniature decorations
Florist's wire
Gold braid or sequins for trimming base
Glue or pins
Plastic film

Select a tree shaped like a pyramid — not one with separate branches. The chain or variety store may have packages of assorted miniature ornaments, such as little angels, Santa Clauses, tiny packages, bugles, etc. Or you can make your own of felt, colored paper, foil, etc.

Unstring glass ornaments and fasten them to tree separately with wire. As you decorate, keep turning tree so that final effect will be equally handsome from every side. Base can be trimmed with gold braid or sequins, glued or pinned in place. When completed, entire tree should be a mass of glittering beauty. Protect finished tree by covering it with plastic film.

More Ideas. Trim tree with spray foam and glitter. Decorate small artificial Christmas wreaths. Dip large pine cones in glue and glitter or decorate each little leaf with ornaments glued in place, to look like tiny Christmas trees. Make table decorations by inserting silvered branches into a slab of plastic foam and decorating these branches. Add artificial holly and small pine cones, candles, or even a toy Santa Claus and reindeer.

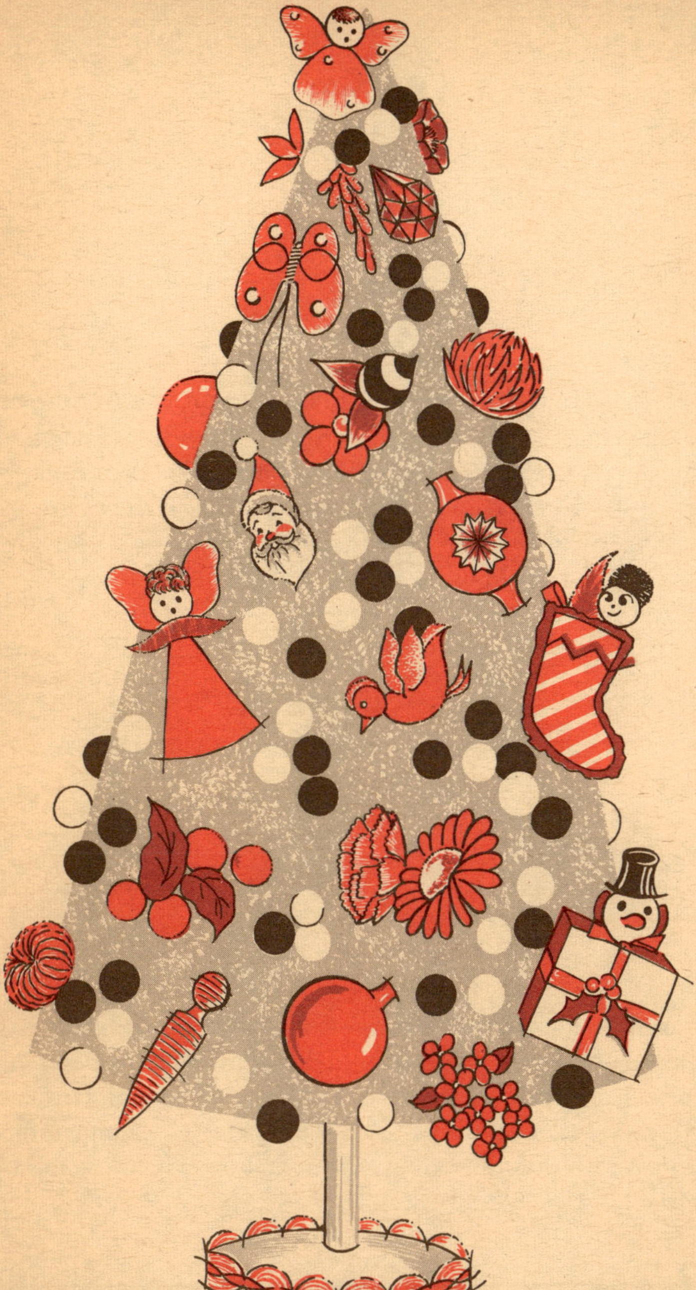

After you've tried making presents, you can decide what to offer for sale. Show samples to your friends and neighbors. When you finally offer something that people really like, you'll know it quickly enough from comments like this:

"Oh, I can think of at least two friends who'd like one of those, and I could use a couple myself."

You're in business!

Help in Finding Materials

Here is a list of manufacturers who supply products used in making the articles described in this book. If you have trouble finding an item in your local stores, write the manufacturer and ask where it is sold. Enclose a self-addressed, stamped envelope. An asterisk preceding a manufacturer's name means that a free booklet is available.

American Crayon Company, 9 Rockefeller Plaza, New York, New York: Prang textile paints.

*American Handicrafts, Advertising Department, 1001 Foch Street, Fort Worth, Texas; arts and crafts materials.

*Borden Chemical Company, 350 Madison Avenue, New York, New York: Elmer's Glue-All, Elmer's cement, Elmer's epoxy.

*Coats & Clark, Inc., 430 Park Avenue, New York, New York: rickrack, sewing and crochet threads, Red Heart yarns, Bondex Iron-On Tape.

*Dow Chemical Company, Consumer Education Dept., Midland, Michigan: Styrofoam, Saran Wrap.

*John Dritz & Sons, 1115 Broadway, New York, New York: magnets, cutting boards, sewing accessories.

East House Industries, 134 Fifth Avenue, New York, New York: gold-paper decorations (Fool's Gold).

*Gurley Novelty Company, 245 Seneca Street, Buffalo, New York: candle-craft materials.

Hero Manufacturing Company, Middleboro, Massachusetts: bag handles, knitting and crochet accessories.

Meyercord Company, 5323 West Lake Street, Chicago, Illinois: decals.

Reynolds Yarns, Inc., 190 Express Street, Plainview, Long Island, New York: yarns, knitting ribbon.

Slomon's Laboratories, Inc., 31-19 Queens Boulevard, Long Island City, New York: Sobo glue.

Walco Products, Inc., 37 West 37th Street, New York, New York: sequins, rhinestones, beads, moving eyes, jewelry-making kits, jewelry cement.

*Wm. E. Wright & Sons, Dept. S-64, West Warren, Massachusetts: braid, tape, rickrack, binding, brocaded ribbon, lace.